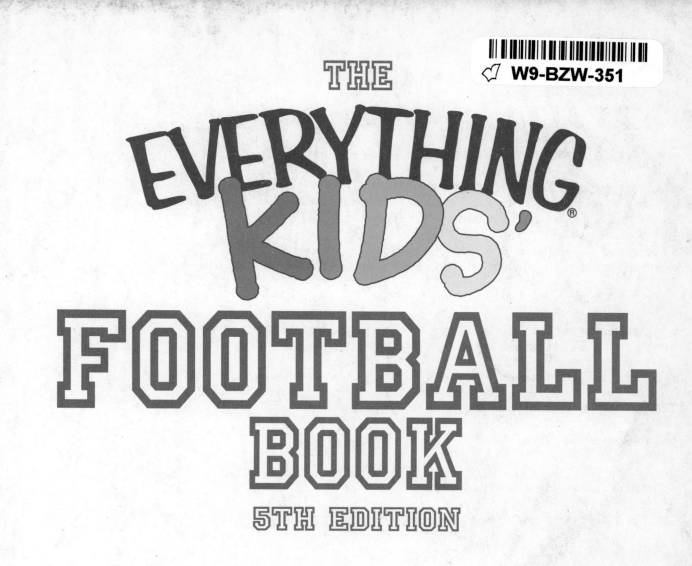

THE EVERYTHING KIDS' FOOTBALL BOOK

5TH EDITION

All-time greats, legendary teams, and today's favorite players—
with tips on playing like a pro

Greg Jacobs

Adams Media
New York London Toronto Sydney New Delhi

Adams Media
An Imprint of Simon & Schuster, Inc.
57 Littlefield Street
Avon, Massachusetts 02322

An Everything® Series Book.
Everything® and everything.com® are registered trademarks of Simon & Schuster, Inc.

ADAMS MEDIA and colophon are trademarks of Simon and Schuster.

For information about special discounts for bulk purchases, please contact Simon & Schuster Special Sales at 1-866-506-1949 or business@simonandschuster.com.

The Simon & Schuster Speakers Bureau can bring authors to your live event. For more information or to book an event contact the Simon & Schuster Speakers Bureau at 1-866-248-3049 or visit our website at www.simonspeakers.com.

Interior illustrations by Kurt Dolber
Puzzles by Beth L. Blair

Manufactured in the United States of America

Printed by LSC Communications, Harrisonburg, VA, U.S.A.

10 9 8 7 6 5
March 2017

ISBN 978-1-4405-9642-1
ISBN 978-1-4405-9643-8 (ebook)

Visit the entire Everything® series at www.everything.com

CONTENTS

ACKNOWLEDGMENTS

I only get a few lines here, so I can't fully express my appreciation to all of these folks. But copious thanks anyway to: Bart and Mary Ann Jacobs, the late Jack Soete, Peter Cashwell, Clint Alexander, Keith Johnson, Gene Ware, David Glover, Brad "Spider" Caldwell, the Penn State football program, Andrea Bell, Kerry Smith, Grace Freedson. And, to my wife and sidekick Burrito Girl, a.k.a. Shari Jacobs, who lets me watch football on the big-screen TV all season. She's the best.

DEDICATION

To Milo, even though he likes baseball, not football . . .

INTRODUCTION

Welcome to the 2016–2017 edition of the wildly popular *The Everything® Kids' Football Book!*

So much has happened in the two years since the last edition came out. The Patriots won their fourth Super Bowl in six appearances this century, continuing their dynasty led by Tom Brady and Bill Belichick. But then the Broncos defeated the Patriots on the way to their own Super Bowl title in Super Bowl 50. College football established a four-team playoff, crowning Ohio State and Alabama as undisputed national champions.

Whether you know a lot about football or hardly anything at all, this book has something to offer you. If you're relatively new to football or if you're looking for new ways to play, Chapter 1 will answer all of your questions. Both long-time and new fans will enjoy the two chapters on professional football and the one on college football. It is easy to find a high school game to watch locally or college and pro games on television. But for the players and coaches, the game itself represents the high point of weeks of preparation. It's not often that a telecast or newspaper report tells fans much about what goes on for a team before game day. But this book can help. Two chapters will give you some insight into the daily efforts of a team: Chapter 5, about high school football, tells you about life around the team, and Chapter 9 talks about the people who make big contributions to the game behind the scenes. In this edition is a description of how scouts and statisticians help teams win, and help fans follow the game. There is also advice on starting and running your very own fantasy football league.

If you've mastered the basics of football or want to learn more about the "Xs and Os," there are two chapters to help you: one about offense and one about defense. Hopefully, this book will be able to teach you something about football, no matter what you already know or don't know. Enjoy!

WORDS to KNOW

NFL: NFL stands for National Football League. The NFL consists of 32 teams across the country that play televised games each Sunday—and sometimes Thursday and Monday—in the fall.

Where Did Football Come From?

In most countries other than the United States, when people talk about football they mean the game we call soccer. Here in the United States, football actually means football, as in the game you play with a brown, oval-shaped ball.

For most of history, people have played games with balls and goals. At least 500 years ago in England, the game we call soccer developed. In soccer, players try to put a round ball into a goal without using their hands.

In the early 1800s, players at the Rugby School in England started cheating. Instead of kicking the ball, they picked it up and ran with it into the goal. Some teams liked to play against the Rugby School—they just tackled whoever picked up the ball! Other teams wanted to play soccer the normal way. Soon two separate forms of the sport were played. In rugby, players were supposed to run with the ball, and defenders were supposed to tackle the ballcarrier to the ground.

Americans picked up the game of rugby, but every team wanted to play by different rules. In the late 1800s, several colleges and athletic clubs in America played games similar to rugby. East Coast universities such as Princeton, Rutgers, Harvard, and Yale eventually got together to try to standardize the rules.

By the turn of the century, American rugby had changed enough that you probably could have recognized the game as football. Every play was a running play. Blockers (without much padding) slammed into each other as hard as they could. There were so many injuries, in fact, that many people tried to ban the sport. At the personal request of President Teddy Roosevelt, Yale athletic director Walter Camp led a commission that created a more exciting and less dangerous game than had been played before. It was Camp who insisted that eleven players was the right number for a team. He invented the idea that the offense had to gain yardage to get a first down. Most importantly, Camp revolutionized football by inventing the forward pass.

College Football

College football in the early 1900s was dominated by the northeastern colleges that are now part of the Ivy League. In fact, it was 1912 before a non–Ivy League school won a national championship. College—not pro—football was the popular spectator sport through the first half of the 1900s. Colleges throughout the country formed teams, and more and more people started watching and playing football. The college bowl games on New Year's Day were the highlight of each season.

In the 1920s, colleges all over the country played football. Professional teams had started playing in the Midwest. Both the pro and college games were well known and well followed. However, football didn't become the big deal that it is now until after the Great Depression and World War II.

Find the Flag

Can you find the seven times the word FLAG is hidden in this game of flag football?

TV Makes Football Popular

By the end of the 1950s, most families had a TV set in their home. Television networks figured out that people loved to watch football. Televised football made the game even more popular and provided a good deal of money for team owners. The Super Bowl, first played in 1967, became the most important sporting event in America. Fans enjoyed watching their favorite college players competing for many years as professionals.

Nowadays, you'll see both college and pro football on TV—college on Saturday, pro on Sunday. Many college teams and almost all pro teams sell out their stadiums every week. High schools and youth leagues stage games each week as well, giving more people a chance to play the game.

Rules of the Game

At first glance, football's rules seem very complicated. The official rulebook is more than 200 pages long. In any game that you watch, you'll probably see at least one play when the announcers aren't quite sure why a referee made a call. But you don't need to understand every little detail to know how to play. Just know the basics, and you'll figure out the complex stuff over the years.

The Simple Rules

A football game consists of four quarters, two in each half. In high school, the quarters are twelve minutes long. In college and in the NFL, the quarters are fifteen minutes long. Whichever team has more points at the end of the four quarters wins.

If the game is tied, the teams usually play overtime. The rules for overtime are different for different levels of play. In the NFL, the teams play a fifth quarter, and whoever scores first wins. At other levels, the teams take turns trying to score from the same spot on the field.

A football field has a 100-yard playing field and two 10-yard end zones. The offense scores points by getting the ball into the other team's end zone, and the defense protects its end zone by keeping the other team as far away from it as possible.

Scoring

In all levels of football there are four ways for the offense to score.

1. **Touchdown**—6 points. Run the ball into the end zone or catch the ball in the end zone.
2. **Extra point**—1 point. After a touchdown, the offense gets one free play. If they kick the ball through the goalposts, they get 1 more point.
3. **Two-point conversion**—2 points. Instead of kicking an extra point after a touchdown, the offense can try to get the ball into the end zone. If they succeed on that play, they get 2 more points.
4. **Field goal**—3 points. Kick the ball through the goalposts.

Offensive Rules

A play starts when the center hikes, or "snaps," the ball between his legs to the quarterback. Until the snap, most of the offensive players must not move. Usually the quarterback does one of two things after the snap:

- He gives the ball to a running back, who runs with the ball behind his blockers.
- He drops back to try to pass the ball to a receiver while the blockers protect him.

In a running play, all of the offensive players are supposed to block. This means that they push the defensive players out of the way so that the running back has room to run. On a passing play, the receivers run down

WORDS to KNOW

PLAY: In soccer or basketball, once the game starts, it keeps going for a long time. In football, once someone is tackled, the game stops for everyone to line up and start again. A play is the action that happens after the ball is hiked and before someone is tackled. Plays can usually be described as passing plays or running plays.

SACK: When the defense tackles the quarterback before he has a chance to pass the ball, that's called a sack. Bruce Smith, who played most of his career for the Buffalo Bills, sacked the quarterback 200 times and holds the all-time NFL record.

OFFENSE AND DEFENSE:

The team of eleven players that controls the ball is the offense. They try to run or pass the ball down the field toward the end zone. The team of eleven players without the ball is the defense. They try to tackle the offensive player with the ball, and they try to knock down or intercept passes.

the field, trying to get open so they can catch a pass, while the linemen stay near the quarterback to block the defenders trying to sack him. If one of the receivers catches the ball, then he can keep running. However, if the ball hits the ground before anyone catches it, that's called an incomplete pass and the offense has to try again from the same spot.

Whether they run or pass, the offense has to keep moving if they want to keep the ball. They have four plays, called downs, to advance 10 yards. If they make the 10 yards, they are awarded a first down, and they keep the ball. If they don't get those 10 yards, then the defense gets the ball.

Fourth down is the offense's last chance to finish gaining their 10 yards to keep the ball. Often, the offense realizes that they're probably not going to get a first down. So they can choose to punt: They kick the ball down the field. The other team then gets the ball, but way farther back than if the offense hadn't punted.

Defensive Rules

The defense, like the offense, is allowed to put eleven players on the field. Unlike the offense, the defense can move around before the snap. On running plays, defensive players are allowed to collide with blockers to knock them out of the way while they try to tackle the ballcarrier. On passing plays, though, there are stricter rules about contact. No one is allowed to interfere with a receiver trying to catch the ball.

The defense's job is to keep the offense from getting a first down. They can do even better, though, by forcing a turnover. If a runner drops the ball, the defense can pick it up and keep the ball. If the defense catches a pass, that's called an interception, and the defense gets to keep the ball.

You Can Play, Too

Most college and professional football players are well over 6 feet tall and weigh more than 200 pounds. You'd never be able to tackle them, even if you and all of your friends tried together. But that doesn't mean you can't play football. Kids' football leagues make sure that everyone, no matter how big or small, can play. How do they do that?

One way of making a game competitive is to be sure that all the players are about the same size. The country's oldest and best-known youth football organization, Pop Warner, takes this approach. Kids as young as five years old can join a team, and there are divisions for kids up to sixteen years old.

Pop Warner teams play tackle football in helmets and pads, and the rules are adjusted a bit for the ages of the players. (For example, the five- to seven-year-olds can play on an 80-yard field.) Games are just like high school games, with ten- to twelve-minute quarters. However, unlike at higher levels of football, in Pop Warner every player must participate in every game. In fact, the rules provide a penalty for teams that don't play all their players.

Pop Warner teams compete in local leagues, usually playing about six to eight games each fall. But the teams start with practice—lots of practice. Each year, players spend a week or so conditioning and then learning the fundamentals of blocking and tackling before they even put on pads. Then, more practices in pads are required. By the time the team is ready for the first game, everyone on the team knows what to do. Football is a complicated game, so the practice time pays off when it's time to compete.

All of the Pop Warner teams nationally are broken into associations of a few local teams each. The winner of an association can advance to playoffs, with each round consisting of the winners of a larger and larger

····· **Football GREAT** ·······

Glenn Scobey "Pop" Warner

Pop Warner was a standout football player at Cornell University who went on to coach college football for forty-five years, starting in 1895. He is the one who had the idea for players to wear numbers, and he also introduced the huddle and many other common football techniques. He supported a youth football league in Philadelphia in the 1930s. The league eventually became the Pop Warner Conference.

FUN FACT

area. With enough wins, a team can even advance to the national tournament in Orlando, Florida. There, the best teams nationwide from each age group play off to crown a national champion. In fact, the midget (eleven- to fifteen-year-old) division final game is usually shown on national television.

Of course, there are other youth football organizations besides Pop Warner. In some areas, each city sponsors teams. There are also police leagues, independent leagues, Boys and Girls Club leagues, county leagues, even leagues of elementary or middle school teams. Most of these leagues operate similarly to Pop Warner—they match players of similar age and size, provide equipment and coaching, and play a weekly schedule.

Skills for Every Type of Player

One of the great things about football is that most anyone can find a position that they're good at, especially on a kids' team. The three most important features of a football player are strength, speed, and football smarts. At your age, all of these skills are best developed by playing a lot. The more games you play, the stronger, faster, and smarter you'll become, just through experience. Older players—starting in high school—put themselves through complex weightlifting or speed training programs. That's important for older players, but until you get to high school, just play as much as you can and you'll find that your body grows into its skills.

When you read the chapters on offense and defense, you'll see the specific skills that are necessary to play each position. If you are one of the fastest folks in your class, then you should try playing receiver or cornerback. If you're one of the biggest or strongest, then you could be a linebacker, a lineman, or a running back. And if you can throw the ball and make quick decisions, you might be an excellent quarterback.

Some people grow stronger, faster, or smarter than others. We can't all have the body of Luke Kuechly or the intelligence of Richard Sherman. You have to remember that you are not yet fully grown. You might think you're too slow to be a receiver. But as your legs get longer and your muscles bigger, your speed will improve. If you know exactly where to throw the ball but your arm is too weak to get the ball there, don't give up the thought of being a quarterback. Keep practicing for a few years, and you could find that all of a sudden your throws are right on target. On that same note, remember that the folks you play against are also not fully grown. If you're the biggest player on your team, you might think that you should stick to playing offensive line or running back. What happens, though, if next year your teammates are all your size or bigger? There's no reason you shouldn't try playing every position, learning the necessary skills, and having fun.

Football Is a Team Game

All this talk about what position you want to play and how you can get better is definitely important, but a football team usually has at least twenty-two players on it. The number one goal is for the team to win. That might mean you have to play your second-favorite position. Your coaches know what's best, and you have to trust them to balance the goals of playing everyone and winning as well.

You might even have to wait your turn to play. If you aren't in the game and your team scores a touchdown, cheer with them just as if you had been playing. Everyone will see what a good sport you are and what a great, positive

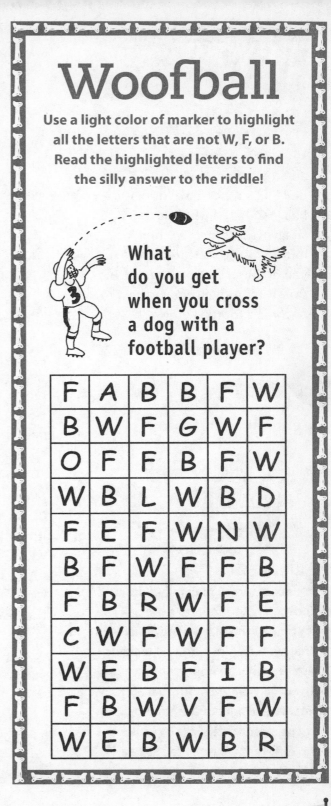

Woofball

Use a light color of marker to highlight all the letters that are not W, F, or B. Read the highlighted letters to find the silly answer to the riddle!

What do you get when you cross a dog with a football player?

F	A	B	B	F	W
B	W	F	G	W	F
O	F	F	B	F	W
W	B	L	W	B	D
F	E	F	W	N	W
B	F	W	F	F	B
F	B	R	W	F	E
C	W	F	W	F	F
W	E	B	F	I	B
F	B	W	V	F	W
W	E	B	W	B	R

attitude you have, even when you don't get to do exactly what you want. Maybe later in the game you'll get your chance. Don't you hope that when you score, your teammates celebrate with you?

Backyard Football

Organized youth football leagues only play one game per week, but you want to play more football than that, right? While a school or community league is the only way to get involved in tackle football with pads and helmets, there's no reason you can't play a scaled-down version of the game on a playground or in your backyard.

Tackling

One noncontact substitute for tackle football is flag football. In flag football, everyone wears a loose belt with ribbons, called flags, on it. Instead of tackling the player with the ball, you pull the flags off of the ballcarrier's belt. Flag football can be played by people of all ages and with all sorts of different rules. In the leagues sponsored by the NFL, teams of five players play on a 50-yard field. In another version of flag football that is played on college campuses, teams of seven players play on an 80-yard field. Of course, you can play anywhere—just put some cones or books on the ground to show where the end zones are.

Probably the most common way to simulate tackle football is to play touch football. When someone touches the ballcarrier with both hands, the play ends. Since no equipment at all is required (other than a ball, of course), touch football is perhaps the most widely played version of the sport.

Blocking

You can avoid tackling people in your backyard by playing touch or flag football, but how do you block? If everyone's about the same size, and especially if most of you have learned proper blocking form, you might just block normally. But a more common method used in flag football is to block like you play defense in basketball: shuffle your feet, and establish a position so that no one can get by you. Then, if someone runs you over, he's committed a foul (like charging in basketball).

You can eliminate the blocking parts of the game altogether. Unless you have a huge number of players, make the rules so the offense usually passes, and make it difficult to rush the quarterback. Here are some ideas.

- **Use a rush count.** This means that anyone who wants to rush the quarterback has to stay at the line of scrimmage and count out loud: "1-Mississippi, 2-Mississippi . . . ." The rusher can cross the line after "5-Mississippi."
- **Make every two completions worth a first down.** You don't have a chain gang on the playground, anyway. Backward passes, or passes thrown behind the line of scrimmage, don't count. This way, the offense is still allowed to run, but they're usually going to pass in order to keep getting first downs.
- **Don't let the quarterback run with the ball unless the defense crosses the line of scrimmage.** Just like you can let the defense blitz once every four downs, you can let the quarterback run once every four downs.
- **Only let defenders who lined up 10 yards behind the line of scrimmage rush the quarterback.** This rule makes the game a bit more like real football, but it still gives the quarterback enough time to throw passes.

Backyard Football for Just a Few Players

Flag and touch football work best with teams of five to seven players. But what if you

TRY THIS

Buy Some Flags!
One way to give yourself the chance to play football more often is to have some flags available in your house. The best kind of flag football belt fastens with Velcro or with a loose clip so that the whole belt comes off when it's yanked. Put a big set of flags in a bag, and bring the bag with you anytime your friends get together.

WORDS to KNOW

LINE OF SCRIMMAGE: The line of scrimmage is where the referee places the ball at the beginning of a play. Neither the offense nor the defense is allowed to cross the line before the ball is snapped and the action begins. Forward passes may only be thrown from behind the line of scrimmage.

BLITZ!: In a regular football game, a "blitz" just means that the defense sends a LOT of players to try to tackle the quarterback. In a playground game with a rush count, though, a blitz just means the defense can rush without counting. Many playground games put a limit on how many times the defense can blitz.

don't have enough for teams that big? Or what if you have an odd number of players so that the teams don't divide evenly?

Dealing with an odd number of players is simple. Make the person who can throw best the steady or all-time quarterback. This player plays quarterback for both teams. If several people want to play quarterback, then rotate who gets to be steady QB every four touchdowns or so.

With teams of three or four, you can use a small field. Put a cone or something at midfield for the first-down marker. Make the rule that you have four plays to get past the cone for a first down, then you have four more plays to score a touchdown.

Kicking Without Goalposts

Unless you are a true football fanatic, you probably don't have goalposts in your backyard. You'll need to change the rule about extra points. Give the team that scores a touchdown one free play. They have the choice of trying for 1 or 2 points:

- If they spot the ball at the 3-yard line, they get 1 point for getting into the end zone on their free play.
- If they instead spot the ball at the 10-yard line, they get 2 points for getting into the end zone.

Field goals are more difficult. You can just make the rule that field goals don't count in your game, so everyone has to try for touchdowns. Or you can put a cone 10 or 20 yards from the end zone, and a team who gets past this cone can automatically choose to take 3 points for kicking a field goal. Another option is to award a field goal for a team that can kick the ball so it lands in a small circle in the end zone. Be creative. You can find all kinds of ways to make field goals part of the game, even if you can't actually kick it through the uprights.

Way to Play

Use the key to decode the football player's answer to the reporter's question!

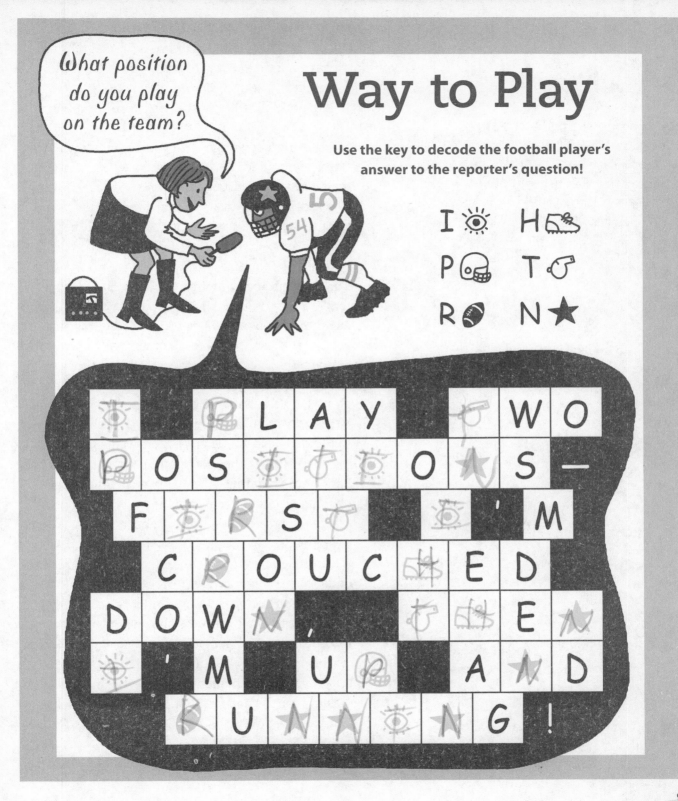

Competitive Football Skill Games

Sometimes you just can't get a real game going when you don't have a lot of people to play. You can still have some football fun, though. Try playing some games similar to drills at a football practice. Here are some ideas:

- **Man-to-man coverage:** The quarterback says "Hike," and a receiver runs out for a pass. One defender tries to intercept or knock down the pass. The receiver gets 1 point for a complete pass, and the defender gets 2 points for an incompletion. Make a time limit of, say, three seconds for the quarterback to release the ball.

- **Target accuracy game:** Set up a bunch of targets—long cones, chairs, or tree trunks work fine. Assign each target a point value, with closer or bigger targets worth less. Put a bunch of footballs in front of a quarterback. Someone says "Go!" and times thirty seconds. The quarterback tries to earn as many points as possible by hitting the targets with the ball. Everyone else races to return the thrown balls to the quarterback. Then it's someone else's turn. See who can get the most points in thirty seconds.

- **Pass pattern game:** This one takes a few more people. Use three receivers and two defenders. The receivers go out for a pass, but they all have to start and stay on only one side of the field. The quarterback has to throw the ball within three seconds. The receiver is down right after catching the ball. Give the offense 1 point for each yard they get on a completion; give the defense 20 points for an incompletion. You can adjust the scoring depending on the size of the field and the skill of the defenders. The offense should be able to win since they outnumber the defense, but a clever and quick defense can do well.

A Brief History of the NFL

In the early days of American football, the best-known teams were college teams, mainly from the Northeast. But in the working-class manufacturing towns of the Midwest, teams from city athletic clubs played hard-fought games against one another. In order to gain an edge against other cities, clubs began paying money to recruit the best players.

In 1920, fourteen teams made up the American Professional Football Association, which was renamed the National Football League two years later. "National" was a funny name for the league, since the teams were only from a small part of the nation.

The All-America Football Conference

The NFL had a very hard time surviving in the 1930s and 1940s. In the Great Depression of the 1930s, many families didn't have enough money to feed themselves, let alone to pay to watch football games. The economy

---

TABLE 2-1

The American Professional Football Association

These were the fourteen teams that started the association that became the NFL. Only one of the teams was located outside the Midwest, and only two of these franchises are still playing today:

Akron Pros	Dayton Triangles
Buffalo All-Americans	Decatur Staleys (still playing as the Chicago Bears)
Canton Bulldogs	Detroit Heralds
Chicago Cardinals (still playing as the Arizona Cardinals)	Hammond Pros
Chicago Tigers	Muncie Flyers
Cleveland Tigers	Rochester Jeffersons
Columbus Panhandles	Rock Island Independents

improved in the early 1940s, but the best football players had to fight in World War II. When the war ended in 1945, huge numbers of athletic young men were returning from military service. People had extra money to spend. The NFL's owners were looking forward to big profits.

But in 1946, a competing league began to play: the All-America Football Conference. The AAFC put teams in many NFL cities, like Chicago and New York.

The NFL refused even to acknowledge the existence of this new league. In fact, when a major sports magazine included the AAFC in a football preview issue, the NFL banned that magazine's writers from its games! But there was no denying that the AAFC was popular. More people were going to AAFC games than to NFL games.

Paul Brown and his scouting staff for the Cleveland Browns did better than any other team in recruiting the most talented young players, and so they ended up dominating the AAFC during its four years of play. The fact that the Browns were so much better than any other team led to the league's downfall, which played its last game in 1949. Three teams from the AAFC—the 49ers, the Browns, and the Baltimore Colts—joined the NFL the next year, while the other teams ceased to exist. It was another decade before the NFL faced another serious challenge from a new football league.

The NFL Championship Game

Before 1933, the NFL held no playoffs, just a regular season. The champion was the team with the best record. In 1932, though, Chicago and Portsmouth were tied for first place. The teams played a one-game playoff to determine the champion. This game was so popular that starting in 1933, the NFL divided its teams into two conferences and planned an NFL championship game between the conference winners. An additional divisional playoff game was played if two teams tied for the top spot in a division. Winning the NFL championship was, for forty-five years,

The First Professional Football Player

In 1892, the Allegheny Athletic Association paid Pudge Heffelfinger $500 to play in a game against the Pittsburgh Athletic Club. That amount of money is equivalent to about $10,000 today. That sounds like a lot, but even a rookie in today's NFL makes nearly $30,000 per game, and most players make a lot more.

The Legendary Paul Brown

Paul Brown was perhaps the best football coach ever. He won state championships at Massillon High School in Ohio. Later, he won national championships with the Ohio State Buckeyes. So when he was appointed as the first head coach of the AAFC's Cleveland Browns, he was already famous— so famous that the NFL's Cleveland Rams left to become the Los Angeles Rams before they would have to compete with the Browns.

the greatest honor in professional football. The Super Bowl didn't exist until the 1966 season.

The NFL kept exactly this format all the way through 1966. In 1967, it divided each conference into two divisions. The division winners played off to determine a conference champion, and the conference champions played in the NFL championship game.

Another New League and Expansion

Professional football reached new heights of popularity in the 1960s. Television networks showed games on Sunday afternoons, exposing more of the country to the game. Pro football finally started to become as important and as well known as college football.

The surge in pro football's popularity made room for other teams. But the successful NFL owners were hesitant to add franchises. So a number of businesspeople, led by Lamar Hunt, formed a new league: the American Football League. The AFL had three major advantages over the leagues that had tried to challenge the NFL before. First, the AFL owners had made their money in other businesses, so if their team lost money at first, they would have some left over. Second, the league signed a network television contract before it even started playing. Television meant that the AFL would get national attention even if its games weren't well attended. And third, the AFL owners held a player draft and shared some of their income with each other. This meant that no single team was likely to dominate the league from year to year and that every team would have a chance to win each game, so people would be interested in watching the games.

Expansion

The NFL, of course, did not like competition. It finally agreed to add a few more teams: The Vikings, Cowboys, Falcons, and Saints all joined the NFL in the 1960s. But the

Lost Player

What's going on? To find out, think of a word that best fits each of the clues. Write the word on the numbered line, then transfer each letter into the grid. Work back and forth between the grid and the clues until you get the silly answer to the riddle!

Why did the football coach shake the vending machine?

1	2		3	4	5	6	7	8		9	10	11
H	E		W	A	N	T	E	d		H	I	S

12	13	14	15	16	17	18		19	20	21	22	
Q	U	A	R	T	E	R		B	A	C	K	!

Where you wear a glove

Hand
9 20 5 8

Opposite of loud

QUIET
12 13 10 2 6

Opposite of dry

WET
3 7 16

Piece of equipment that stops a car

Brake
19 15 14 22 17

What happens when a car doesn't stop

crash
21 18 4 11 1

Football GREAT

The Undefeated 1972 Dolphins

In 1972, the Miami Dolphins became the first team to win every game in a season. The team capped its 14-0 regular season with three postseason victories, including a 14-7 victory over the Redskins in Super Bowl VII. Members of the 1972 Dolphins still celebrate together each season after the last undefeated team loses a game.

AFL expanded too, adding the Miami Dolphins and the Cincinnati Bengals. Teams were offering more and more money to players, trying to get them to switch leagues.

Chiefs owner Lamar Hunt and Cowboys owner Tex Schramm led a campaign to merge the two leagues into an expanded NFL. They agreed to play a championship game between the AFL and NFL winners starting after the 1966 season, which was the beginning of the Super Bowl. In 1970, the two leagues joined. There were ten AFL teams and sixteen NFL teams, so the Baltimore Colts, Cleveland Browns, and Pittsburgh Steelers agreed to join AFL teams in the new American Football Conference, the AFC. The remaining thirteen teams formed the National Football Conference.

A few years after Hunt and Schramm's agreement, most people thought the NFL to be a far better league than the AFL. In the first two AFL-NFL championship games, the NFL's Green Bay Packers soundly defeated their AFL opponents. NFL fans and owners wondered whether agreeing to play against such bad teams had been a smart move. But in the third AFL-NFL championship game (in what is now known as Super Bowl III), the AFL's New York Jets beat the NFL's Baltimore Colts by 9 points, even though the Colts had been favored to win by more than two touchdowns. The AFL's Kansas City Chiefs blew out the NFL's Minnesota Vikings in Super Bowl IV after the 1969 season. When it came time in 1970 for the leagues to actually merge, they did so as equals.

Bigger and Bigger and Bigger

The NFL was not done expanding. In 1976, the Seattle Seahawks and the Tampa Bay Buccaneers joined the league, the Carolina Panthers and Jacksonville Jaguars joined in 1995, and the Houston Texans were created in 2002. But expansion was about more than just adding new teams in new cities. After the merger, the NFL set about to grow in every possible way.

For a long time before 1960, NFL teams played twelve games in their regular season. That number increased to fourteen games per season in 1961. In 1978, the sixteen-game season that is still played today began.

Starting with the merger in 1970, the playoffs were expanded to ten teams: six division winners and four wild card teams. In 1990, two more wild card teams allowed twelve teams in the playoffs. More playoff games meant more television money and more big events. The NFL season, which used to be completely over in December, stretched into late January.

More Teams, More Games, More Playoffs

NFL expansion created new and more dedicated fans. Every city wanted a team, but the NFL couldn't just add an unlimited number of teams. Cities started convincing owners to move their teams. The Oakland Raiders moved to Los Angeles in 1982, though they moved back to Oakland in 1995. Before the 1984 season, the Baltimore Colts moved to Indianapolis in the middle of the night. The St. Louis Cardinals became the Arizona Cardinals in 1988, but St. Louis got a new team in 1995 when the Rams relocated there. The Houston Oilers moved to Tennessee to become the Titans in 1997. The Cleveland Browns moved to Baltimore in 1995 to become the Ravens, and a new Browns team was created in 1999.

Why did all these teams move? In most cases, the new city offered the owner a brand new stadium and lots of money. These new stadiums were more comfortable than the old ones and included more luxury boxes. The new cities had plenty of folks willing to pay enormous amounts of money for season tickets, and plenty of rich people or companies ready to pony up for the luxury

WORDS to KNOW

THE MERGER: Officially, the AFL merged with the NFL in 1970, even though they had played championship games since the 1966 season. You will often hear broadcasters refer to events "since the merger." Though team and individual statistics before 1970 are official and do count in the record books, the year of the merger represents when the NFL started to resemble the league you watch today.

WILD CARD: Before 1970, the only teams in the playoffs were the division winners. In the 1970 season, the two teams in each conference with the best records that were not division winners were invited to the playoffs. These teams played each other in the wild card game. The winner of that game advanced to play a division winner.

WORDS to KNOW

BLACKOUT: In the first years of televised football, a team's home games weren't allowed to be shown on TV in that team's city. The games were blacked out because the league worried that fans wouldn't go to the game if they could just watch at home. In 1973, Congress passed a law that the game had to be shown on TV if it was sold out ahead of time. That law still holds today. Since most games are sold out now, blackouts are rare.

boxes. Owners found that by even threatening to move to a new city, their original city would often build a new stadium just to keep the team from moving. In 2015, fourteen of the NFL's thirty-two teams played in a stadium that had been built in this century; all but about five played in a stadium that was probably built in your parents' lifetime. And even more moves and new stadiums are planned. Los Angeles hasn't had a team since the Rams and Raiders moved out; however, as of 2015, three or more teams are hoping to move to play in a brand-new stadium there.

Television, Satellite TV, and the Internet

One final area of growth for the NFL came from television and other media coverage. The year 1970 marked the debut of *Monday Night Football*, which was among the most watched television programs every week. For a long

Find the Football

Find the one time that FOOT-BALL is spelled correctly. Look up and down, side to side, and backwards!

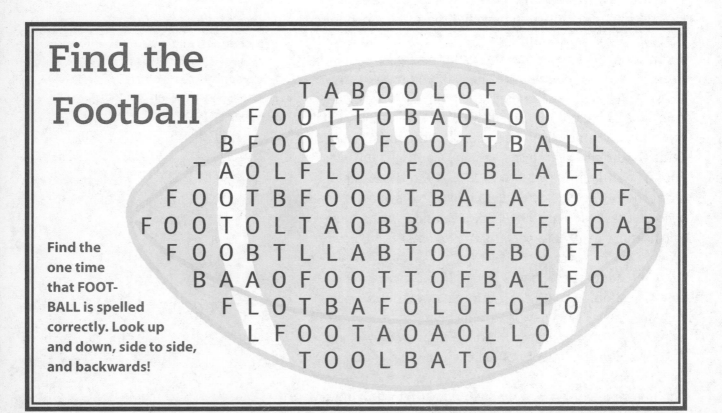

```
      T A B O O L O F
    F O O T T O B A O L O O
  B F O O F O F O O T T B A L L
  T A O L F L O O F O O B L A L F
  F O O T B F O O O T B A L A L O O F
  F O O T O L T A O B B O L F L F L O A B
  F O O B T L L A B T O O F B O F T O
  B A A O F O O T T O F B A L F O
  F L O T B A F O L O F O T O
  L F O O T A O A O L L O
    T O O L B A T O
```

time, you could watch only three games per weekend: two games on Sunday and one on Monday night.

In the mid-1990s, the NFL made it possible for fans to watch all of its games. If they pay lots of money, fans with a special kind of satellite TV can choose to watch any game being played. In the mid-2000s, a satellite radio service made it possible to listen to all of the games on radio. It is possible now to watch some games online. The NFL Network, a cable channel owned by the league itself, began in 2003. It broadcasts behind-the-scenes footage, studio shows, and some live games.

The Biggest Event in America: The Super Bowl

The AFL-NFL championship game was named the "Super Bowl" by Chiefs owner Lamar Hunt. Super indeed. After more than fifty years, Super Bowl Sunday is an unofficial national holiday. The game has become much more than just a league championship. Many Americans—at least one-third of the population—watch the game on television, and many people throw parties and watch with their friends and families.

The last few Super Bowls have been watched by well over 100 million people. The only sporting event in the world that is more significant is soccer's World Cup.

Super Bowls are numbered starting with Super Bowl I after the 1966 season. This is because the regular season lasts from September through December, but the championship game isn't played until the next year. The New England Patriots won the Super Bowl in 2015, but they were the champions of the season that was played in the fall of 2014.

I. Packers 35, Chiefs 10. This was the first AFL-NFL championship game, but it wasn't yet called the Super Bowl.

II. Packers 33, Raiders 14. Packers coach Vince Lombardi won his last world championship.

Brush Up

This coach is giving one of his players a compliment—or is he?
To find out what the coach is saying, you must write all the letters
from the scattered pieces into their proper spaces in the grid.
Hint: Try matching the pattern of the black boxes!

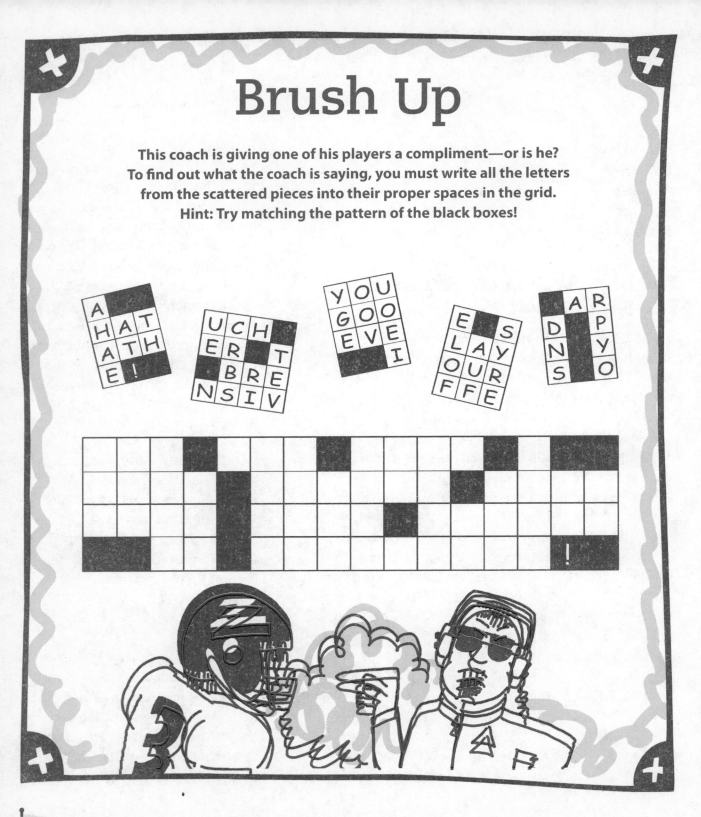

III. Jets 16, (Baltimore) Colts 7. Joe Namath's Jets showed everyone that the AFL was just as good as the NFL.

IV. Chiefs 23, Vikings 7.

V. (Baltimore) Colts 16, Cowboys 13. Chuck Howley of the Cowboys was voted the game's most valuable player, even though his team lost.

VI. Cowboys 24, Dolphins 3.

VII. Dolphins 14, Redskins 7. The 1972 Dolphins became the first team in NFL history to complete an undefeated season.

VIII. Dolphins 24, Vikings 7. The Dolphins were the first team to appear in the Super Bowl three years in a row.

IX. Steelers 16, Vikings 6. The Vikings lost their third of four Super Bowls.

X. Steelers 21, Cowboys 17. The Steelers came from behind with two touchdowns in the fourth quarter, then intercepted a pass on the last play of the game.

XI. Raiders 32, Vikings 14. Raiders head coach and Hall of Famer John Madden won his only Super Bowl.

XII. Cowboys 27, Broncos 10.

XIII. Steelers 35, Cowboys 31. The Steelers won again in the matchup of the greatest teams of the 1970s.

XIV. Steelers 31, (Los Angeles) Rams 19. The Steelers won their fourth Super Bowl in four tries.

XV. Raiders 27, Eagles 10.

XVI. 49ers 26, Bengals 21. San Francisco quarterback Joe Montana led his team to a 20-0 halftime lead. The San Francisco defense forced five turnovers.

XVII. Redskins 27, Dolphins 17. Washington quarterback Joe Theismann won his only Super Bowl.

XVIII. (Los Angeles) Raiders 38, Redskins 9. This would be the last victory for the AFC for fourteen years.

Football GREAT

Joe Namath
Jets quarterback Joe Namath "guaranteed" that his team would win Super Bowl III, even though the Colts were heavily favored. Namath proved the media and the analysts wrong and earned the MVP award in the game. He was one of professional football's first superstars, appearing in movies and TV shows when he wasn't playing football.

WORDS to KNOW

DEFLATEGATE: After the Patriots beat the Colts 45-7 in the 2014 AFC Championship game, the Colts claimed that the Patriots were using underinflated footballs. The NFL claimed to find that the footballs used that day were not fully inflated. But footballs, like balloons and tires, should lose pressure on cold days—scientists call this the "ideal gas law." It's still unclear what exactly happened, but it certainly gave reporters lots and lots to talk about.

Eureka!

Gold was discovered in California in 1848, and large numbers of gold diggers flocked to the West Coast starting in 1849. The new arrivals were nicknamed 49ers. Nearly 100 years later, the All-America Football League created a franchise in San Francisco, and the team took on the 49ers name. Sourdough Sam, the 49ers mascot, is a cheerful football-loving gold digger.

NATIONAL CHAMPIONS

XIX.   49ers 38, Dolphins 16. In his only Super Bowl appearance, Miami quarterback Dan Marino lost to Joe Montana's 49ers.

XX.   Bears 46, Patriots 10. Coach Mike Ditka led his overwhelming favorite Bears to a convincing victory.

XXI.   Giants 39, Broncos 20. Giants coach Bill Parcells won his first of three Super Bowl appearances.

XXII.   Redskins 42, Broncos 10. Skins quarterback Doug Williams not only became the first black quarterback in the Super Bowl, but he was the game's MVP.

XXIII.   49ers 20, Bengals 16. Joe Montana threw the winning TD to John Taylor with 34 seconds remaining, but 49ers receiver Jerry Rice was the MVP.

XXIV.   49ers 55, Broncos 10. Ho-hum, Joe Montana won his fourth Super Bowl and his third MVP award.

XXV.   Giants 20, Bills 19. Scott Norwood's 47-yard field goal attempt went wide right as time expired.

XXVI.   Redskins 37, Bills 24.

XXVII.   Cowboys 52, Bills 17. Dallas quarterback Troy Aikman won his first of three Super Bowls.

XXVIII.   Cowboys 30, Bills 13. The Bills tied the Vikings and the Broncos with four Super Bowl appearances and four losses.

XXIX.   49ers 49, Chargers 26. This time the 49ers were led by quarterback Steve Young, who threw six touchdowns.

XXX.   Cowboys 27, Steelers 17.

XXXI.   Packers 35, Patriots 21. QB Brett Favre led a resurgence of the Packers franchise, which had not seen such good times since the days of coach Vince Lombardi.

XXXII.   Broncos 31, Packers 24. Though the Broncos had lost four previous Super Bowls, they won this time behind a tremendous rushing attack.

XXXIII.   Broncos 34, Falcons 19. Quarterback John Elway won his second straight Super Bowl and the MVP trophy as well.

Perfect Play

Give yourself six points if you can match this touchdown to its perfect shadow!

XXXIV. Rams 23, Titans 16. The Titans had one last play from the 10-yard line, but Mike Jones tackled receiver Kevin Dyson at the 1-yard line to seal the game.

XXXV. Ravens 34, Giants 7. The Ravens defense dominated this game, allowing only a special teams touchdown.

XXXVI. Patriots 20, Rams 17. Kicker Adam Vinatieri nailed a 48-yard field goal to end the game. First-year starting quarterback Tom Brady was MVP.

XXXVII. Buccaneers 48, Raiders 21. The Tampa defense intercepted quarterback Rich Gannon five times, returning three for touchdowns.

XXXVIII. Patriots 32, Panthers 29. Once again Adam Vinatieri won the game with a last-second field goal, and once again quarterback Tom Brady was the MVP.

XXXIX. Patriots 24, Eagles 21. Vinatieri, Brady, and coach Bill Belichick won another close game.

XL. Steelers 21, Seahawks 10. Receiver Hines Ward and running back Jerome Bettis were the offensive heroes of the Steelers, who had just barely made the playoffs.

XLI. Colts 29, Bears 17. Peyton Manning, who had been a top-rated quarterback for seven years without a championship, showed he could come through in a big game.

XLII. Giants 17, Patriots 14. David Tyree's famous "helmet catch" helped defeat New England, who had not lost a game all year until the Super Bowl.

XLIII. Steelers 27, Cardinals 23. The game ended with an amazing touchdown pass to MVP Santonio Holmes in the back corner of the end zone.

XLIV. Saints 31, Colts 17. Saints quarterback and MVP Drew Brees led a come-from-behind victory against the favored Colts.

XLV. Packers 31, Steelers 25. MVP Aaron Rodgers puts on a show as the Packers' latest franchise quarterback.

XLVI. Giants 21, Patriots 17. Eli Manning won the Super Bowl for the second time, once more than his brother Peyton, and just once fewer than his rival Tom Brady.

XLVII. Ravens 34, 49ers 31. The 49ers *almost* came back from way behind after a power outage at the Superdome that stopped the game for half an hour.

XLVIII. Seahawks 43, Broncos 8. The Seahawks scored a safety on the game's first play. Denver quarterback Peyton Manning never did figure out Seattle's smothering defense.

XLIX. Patriots 28, Seahawks 24. It looked like the Seahawks would win after a miracle catch by Jermaine Kearse. On the 1-yard line, Seattle tried to throw a pass for the winning TD, but Malcolm Butler's amazing interception sealed the game for New England.

50. Broncos 24, Panthers 10. The Broncos' defense, led by Von Miller and DeMarcus Ware, harassed Panthers quarterback Cam Newton all night, causing an interception and two fumbles.

Who Are These Teams, Anyway?

Nowadays, the NFL's thirty-two teams are divided into two conferences: the American Football Conference (AFC) and the National Football Conference (NFC). These conferences can be traced back in league history to the AFL-NFL merger in 1970. The AFC consists mainly of old AFL teams, and the NFC consists mainly of original NFL teams. Each conference is broken into four divisions with four teams in each division.

How Do You Figure Out a Team's Schedule?

Each team plays sixteen regular season games. With thirty-two teams, it's not possible for a team to play every other team in a season. Instead, each team plays a schedule that depends on what division they're in, with most of the opponents changing from year to year.

TABLE 3-1

AFC East	AFC West	AFC North	AFC South
New England Patriots	Denver Broncos	Cincinnati Bengals	Indianapolis Colts
New York Jets	Kansas City Chiefs	Pittsburgh Steelers	Tennessee Titans
Miami Dolphins	San Diego Chargers	Baltimore Ravens	Jacksonville Jaguars
Buffalo Bills	Oakland Raiders	Cleveland Browns	Houston Texans
NFC East	**NFC West**	**NFC North**	**NFC South**
Philadelphia Eagles	Seattle Seahawks	Green Bay Packers	Carolina Panthers
Dallas Cowboys	San Francisco 49ers	Chicago Bears	New Orleans Saints
New York Giants	Arizona Cardinals	Detroit Lions	Atlanta Falcons
Washington Redskins	Los Angeles Rams	Minnesota Vikings	Tampa Bay Buccaneers

For example, here's how the NFC North's Green Bay Packers schedule breaks down in 2016.

- Two games each against the other teams in their division: So they play the Vikings twice, the Bears twice, and the Lions twice.
- One game each against the teams in the NFC East: the Cowboys, Giants, Eagles, and Washington.
- One game each against the teams in the AFC South: the Texans, Jaguars, Colts, and Titans.
- Since the Packers finished second in their division in 2015, in 2016 they get to play two more games against other NFC teams who also came in second: that would be the Seahawks and the Eagles.

In 2017, the Packers will play their division games, the NFC South, the AFC North, and two NFC games that depend on where the Packers finish in their division.

Playoffs

After the sixteen-game season, the best teams get to play in the playoffs. In playoff games, whichever team wins gets to play again the next week, and the losing team is done for the season. The last playoff game is the Super Bowl, and the winning team is the NFL champion.

A total of twelve of the thirty-two teams, six in each conference, make the playoffs. Figuring out which teams get into the playoffs isn't easy. Here are the guidelines:

- The winning team in each division makes the playoffs.
- In each conference, the two teams with the best records that aren't division winners also make the playoffs. These two teams are called wild card teams.

Once the playoff teams are determined, the play-off schedule is set. The first weekend after the regular season is wild card weekend. The wild card teams play against four of the eight division-winning teams. The two

Tiebreakers

The hard part of figuring out who's in the playoffs comes when teams finish the season with the same record. The NFL tiebreaker rules are quite complicated. Games within a division and games between teams in the same conference are most important when determining who wins a tiebreaker. You can read the details at *www.nfl.com*.

Preseason Games

Starting in August, each team plays four preseason games. These do not count in the standings, so the best players don't usually play much. Instead, you'll see some of the backup players competing for jobs.

FUN FACT

Oakland's Coaching Carousel

Most head coaches are allowed a few years to try and build a winning football team. When a coach stays with a team for a long time, he provides stability, discipline, and a winning program that the players like. However, the Oakland Raiders have had ten head coaches since the turn of the century! In contrast, the Patriots have had only one head coach during that time.

teams in each conference with the best records earn a bye, meaning they don't have to play a game during wild card weekend. Instead, they get an extra week off.

After wild card weekend comes the divisional play-offs, in which the teams with byes play the winners from wild card weekend. In the next weekend, the winners play the conference championship games, after which only two teams are left—the AFC champion and the NFC champion. These are the teams that go to the Super Bowl.

The Bosses

Have you ever heard television reporters talk about a team's power structure? They don't mean the offensive line. Though the players play the games, there's a whole group of people on every team who determine which players play and how they play. A team's power structure consists of, among others, the coach, the general manager, and the owner.

The Coach

The head coach is responsible for preparing his team for each game. In the game itself, the head coach makes strategic decisions, like whether to punt or to try for a first down. NFL football is so complicated that a head coach can't run everything alone. The head coach hires a large number of assistants, who take charge of smaller aspects of the team. For example, the linebacker coach teaches the linebackers how to play their positions, and the defensive coordinator coaches the entire defense and is in charge of each week's defensive game plan.

At first glance, coaching seems pretty easy. It's the players who have to run and tackle, and the coaches just watch, right? But coaching is exhausting in a different way. Coaches watch game film all the time. They look at their next opponent, trying to find weaknesses. They look at their own games, evaluate players, and figure out how to make their own guys more successful. Players show up at practice, work hard, and go home when they're done. Coaches prepare for practice just like a teacher prepares for class. Once practice is over, the coach goes right back to preparing.

A winning NFL team requires great players as well as great coaching. It's not always fair to judge a coach as good or bad based on his record in one or two seasons. Yet it's reasonable to say that the best coaches are those who have led their teams to the playoffs many times over the years. For example, one of the best NFL coaches today is Andy Reid of the Kansas City Chiefs. Reid coached the Eagles for fourteen years, taking the Eagles to the playoffs in nine of those seasons and winning 58 percent of his games. Even successful coaches get fired—the Eagles let Reid go after a losing season in 2012, but the Chiefs picked him up the next year. Under his leadership, the Chiefs became a playoff team.

The General Manager (GM)

The coaches figure out what to do with their players. But a coach can't just ask any old player to join his team. A team must first sign that player to a contract and agree to pay him a salary. It is the general manager's job to find and sign players to fill out the team.

This is a more complicated job than you might think. Each team is only allowed to spend a certain amount of money each year. This "salary cap" means that if a star player wants a lot of money, the general manager either needs to let that player go to another team, get rid of another player, or pay other team members less so that he can afford to sign the star. If a general manager wants a player who is already signed to a contract by another team, the GM has to make a trade. Perhaps the

Football GREAT

Coach Bill Belichick

Belichick began his NFL coaching career with the Detroit Lions and Denver Broncos. However, his first successful stint came under head coach Bill Parcells with the New York Giants where he won two Super Bowls as the team's defensive coordinator. In 2000 he became the head coach of the New England Patriots, leading them to the playoffs in thirteen of sixteen years, to six Super Bowl appearances, and four Super Bowl victories. He is currently the longest-tenured head coach in the NFL, and has won over 70 percent of his games with the Patriots, the best in the NFL.

most visible part of a GM's job comes on draft day, when each team's GM takes turns picking former college players to be part of their teams. Figuring out which players to draft requires serious scouting and research. The NFL draft is shown on national television so that fans everywhere can see the decisions each team makes right away.

On just a very few teams, the head coach also serves as the general manager. Doing both jobs requires a lot of work for one person. Most teams want different people in those two roles, partly to give each person more time to concentrate on the job, and partly to give two different points of view to the construction of the team.

Fractured Football

The linebacker hit this football so hard it was broken in half! Which two pieces will fit together to make one complete ball?

The Owners

Head coaches and GMs worked for many years at lower-level football jobs. These folks proved their worth before being hired to such an important position. No matter how good coaches or GMs become, though, they're not going to work their way up to become owners. The owner of a franchise is simply the person who bought the team. Football knowledge isn't required to buy an NFL team, but having a lot of money is. For example, Dan Snyder bought the Washington team in 1999 for $750 million. In 2014, it was estimated that he could sell the franchise again for about three times that price. *Forbes* magazine's research suggests that the average NFL team is worth more than a billion dollars, with the Cowboys the highest-valued team at more than $3 billion.

An ideal owner buys the team, hires a strong GM and an outstanding coach, and lets THEM make all the football decisions. If the GM or the coach isn't performing well, it is the owner alone who has the power to fire them. That's often a difficult decision for an owner, especially an owner who knows little about the ins and outs of an NFL team. If the team didn't make the playoffs this year, is it because the GM did a poor job of obtaining players? Were the players good enough but poorly coached? Or was it a really good team that just hit a few bad breaks and will be very good next year? It's usually quite hard to tell the difference. Since it's easier to fire the coach than to fire all the players, the coach is very often the one who pays the price for a bad season.

Be a Part of the Action

Most NFL stadiums have room for about 70,000 people. Being one of those 70,000, all cheering at the top of their lungs for the home team to win, is an experience that you will treasure for a long time. If you get a chance to go, be sure to look around you, see everything that is happening, and really savor the trip.

FUN FACT

Shopping for Players?

Some coaches are willing to put in the extra work to gain the extra control of being able to sign *AND* coach players. As legendary coach Bill Parcells once said, "If they want you to cook the dinner, at least they ought to let you shop for some of the groceries."

How Long Do Coaches Last?

Washington has had eight different head coaches in the sixteen years since Dan Snyder bought the team. On the other hand, the Pittsburgh Steelers are on only their third coach since the AFL-NFL merger in 1970.

**Wolves
vs
Bears**

Saturday,
November 20
1:00 PM
Cubs Stadium

Section 115
Row 2, Seat 5

Good for one admission.
Event takes place rain or shine.

7650090 231356

WORDS to KNOW

TAILGATING: A tailgate party is a picnic in the stadium parking lot before a game. This can be as simple as eating some sandwiches out of a cooler while sitting on the back of your car. Elaborate tailgaters bring lawn chairs, big grills, and four-course meals. Part of the fun is being with all the other tailgating fans of your team. Bring extra food to share, and you'll meet some interesting folks!

Getting Tickets

Ticket prices for NFL games are very, very high. It costs an average of $85 for just one ticket to one game, and that's for an average ticket in an average-priced stadium. A premium ticket to a New England Patriots game costs more than $500!

To get tickets, go to *www.nfl.com* and click "tickets." Then click on the team whose game you want to go to. You'll read how to purchase the tickets you want. Most NFL tickets are sold as season tickets. To get a season ticket, you pay the team an upfront "personal seat license" fee, you pay the team for ten tickets, and you get to sit in the same seat for all eight regular season home games and for the two preseason home games.

Very often, it's just impossible to buy tickets for a team's games. The tickets were sold years in advance. For example, the Arizona Cardinals not only sell all their season tickets every year, they also have thousands of people on a waiting list. So how can you go to a game? The other way to go is to find a friend or relative who has season tickets. Sometimes, season ticket holders can't go to all the games, so they'll give away (or sell at face value) their seats to one or two games. The NFL also has an online ticket exchange, where you might be able to grab a couple of tickets a few days before the game. Be careful—don't buy an NFL ticket from someone you don't know and trust. Most teams do not allow tickets to be sold for more than face value. Furthermore, tickets that look real might be fake. Tickets have bar codes on them that tell the computer who bought the ticket. If your ticket doesn't check out with the computer, you won't be allowed in.

At the Game

Before you go, ask someone or look online for advice about getting to the stadium. With 70,000 people trying to cram into one building, crowds can get huge and lines can get long. Find out where to park and if there's a better way to get to the stadium than by car.

Also, read up on stadium rules about what you can bring with you. No backpacks are allowed at NFL games, but you can bring a small, clear-sided bag with things like water, sunscreen, a poncho, a hat, and sunglasses.

The game will definitely be exciting, causing you and all the fans to cheer, yell, scream, and jump out of your seats. That's exactly what's supposed to happen! Be sure to be considerate of others while you're cheering, though. You—and the other fans—don't need to use foul language, throw things, or be obnoxious to fans of the visiting team. Cheer as loud as you can for your team, but don't be rude and ruin someone else's experience.

Watch for parts of the game you can't see on TV. You'll notice parts of football that the narrow television screen can't show you. Before the game and during half-time, walk around. Most stadiums have murals, statues, or wall hangings honoring the team's history. Talk to some fans in the concession line and find out where they're from, what they know about the team, and how long they've been fans. You're at an NFL game, one of the greatest possible American cultural experiences—make the most of it!

If You Can't Go

You can watch virtually any NFL game on television if you can't go to the game. Watching on TV is a less intense experience, but it is a lot more convenient (and a lot cheaper, too). Near a city, the home team's games will almost always be shown on local network channels. If you want to watch an out-of-town team, you may have to watch on cable or satellite.

Most NFL games are played on Sunday afternoons. The local CBS station will pick AFC games and the local FOX station will pick NFC games. On Sunday night, one special game will be shown on NBC to the entire country, announced by Al Michaels and Cris Collinsworth.

TRY THIS

Dressing Up
You don't have to wear a Halloween-style costume to an NFL game, but it is sometimes fun. Look at the fans around the stadium. Many will be wearing team jerseys, of course. But a few will have elaborate outfits with special hats or painted faces. Dressing up adds to the fun!

Be Prepared!
NFL games go on in 100-degree heat as well as in heavy snow. Check the forecast ahead of time, and bring anything you think you might need. It's better to have a pair of gloves in your bag that you never use than to spend three hours at the game with frozen hands, wishing you had brought the gloves!

Football Fill In

Get ready to pass, punt, and run! If you're a rookie player, you can choose from the answer words scattered around the puzzle on the next page. Pro ball players should be able to complete the puzzle without looking!

ACROSS

2. A six-point score earned when the ball crosses the goal line
6. Player who receives the snap during a field goal attempt
9. Fake grass sometimes used in football stadiums
11. Area created by the offensive line to protect the quarterback
13. Offensive players who catch passes
14. A person or animal that represents a team
15. To throw the ball
17. A football field has 100 of these
18. Person who makes sure the teams follow the rules
21. Three points earned when ball is kicked through the goalpost
24. Arena where football games are played
25. People who cheer for a team
26. Offensive player who throws passes

DOWN

1. Person on the sideline who guides the team through plays
3. A group of players who gather together to discuss the next play
4. What the referee blows to stop a play
5. Offensive player who snaps the ball
7. Players who control the ball and try to score
8. What the fans eat in the stands
10. A group of football players who work together
12. One way to stop a player from running
16. What a player wears to protect his head
19. Game played where the school's graduates come to watch
20. A defensive player who tries to keep receivers from catching passes
21. What a referee throws to indicate a foul
22. Players who keep the other team from scoring
23. When more than four defensive players rush the quarterback

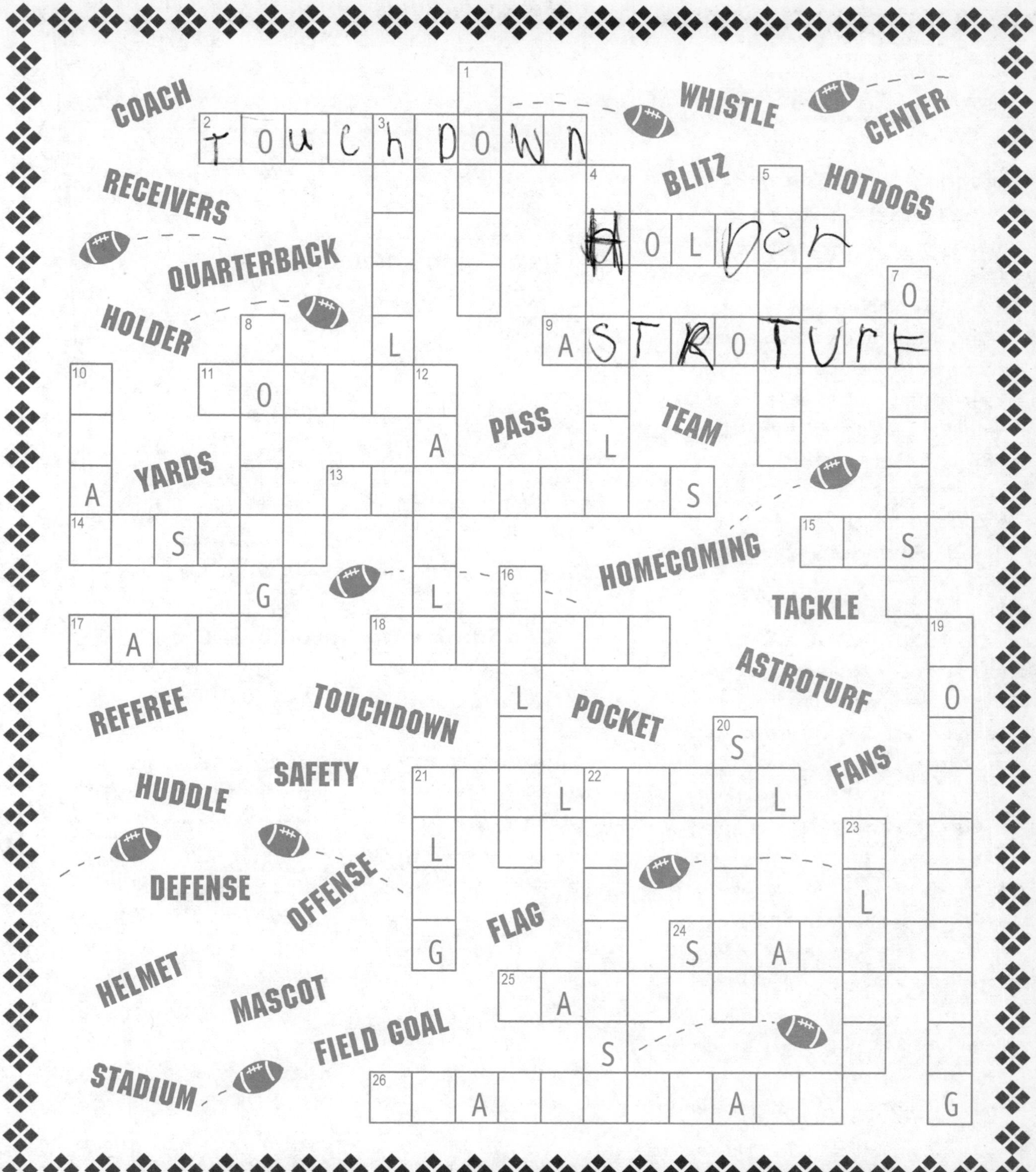
COACH
WHISTLE
CENTER
RECEIVERS
BLITZ
HOTDOGS
QUARTERBACK
HOLDER
PASS
TEAM
YARDS
HOMECOMING
TACKLE
ASTROTURF
REFEREE
TOUCHDOWN
POCKET
SAFETY
FANS
HUDDLE
DEFENSE
OFFENSE
FLAG
HELMET
MASCOT
FIELD GOAL
STADIUM

Monday Night Football

In the 1960s and 1970s, no more than two games were shown on TV each Sunday. In 1970, ABC started showing one game every Monday night, using their best announcers and lots of cameras and graphics to produce a big show. *Monday Night Football* lasted until 2005 on ABC, and every week it was one of the top ten most-watched TV shows. Now, MNF is on ESPN with the announcing team of Mike Tirico and Jon Gruden.

The *Heidi* Game

At 7:00 P.M. on November 17, 1968, the Jets took a 5-point lead on the Raiders with sixty-five seconds to go. Though a football game usually takes only about three hours to play, this one was taking longer. NBC television had planned to air the movie *Heidi* at 7:00, so they stopped showing the football game and showed the movie. Fans, especially in New York, were furious. So many people called NBC to complain that NBC issued an apology and changed their rules to show all football games to the end.

Sunday Rituals

The best part of watching your team on TV is that you don't have to make a big trip to still feel like you're at the game. Fans love to watch with a group of friends. You can all have lunch together before the game or put out a bunch of snacks to eat during the game. The best part is, you get to do it all again for the next week's game!

The Commentators

At the stadium, an announcer will give the crowd game information, such as who carried the ball, how many yards he gained, and who made the tackle. That's it.

On TV, though, two or three people talk all through the game. One, called the play-by-play announcer, states the basic game information. The others, called color commentators or analysts, just talk about football throughout the game. Good color analysts can teach you about the game, show you the little details that made a play work or not work, and tell you a bit about the players.

The Sunday Night Football Crew

The best-known television announcing team today works the Sunday night games: Al Michaels and Cris Collinsworth. Michaels is known as the best play-by-play announcer for any sport. He started his career as a baseball announcer and became famous in 1980 when he called the U.S. hockey team's Olympic upset of the Soviet Union with, "Do you believe in miracles? Yes!" He has worked prime-time NFL football since 1986.

Collinsworth spent eight seasons as a Pro Bowl–quality wide receiver for the Cincinnati Bengals, helping lead the team to two Super Bowls. After he retired in 1989, he began getting more and more jobs as a broadcaster. He is best known for his insightful and specific analysis of football strategy. He has a talent for explaining quickly and clearly why a play worked or didn't work. Collinsworth is currently one of the best teachers of the game on television.

Chapter 4
COLLEGE FOOTBALL

Football GREAT

Emmitt Smith

Running back Emmitt Smith is best known for his thirteen years with the Dallas Cowboys, during which he helped lead the team to three Super Bowl victories. Because Emmitt was so successful in the pros, many fans forget his outstanding career at the University of Florida, which earned him a place in the College Football Hall of Fame. After Emmitt began playing in the NFL, he continued to take classes. In 1996, six years after he began his NFL career, he graduated with a degree in public recreation.

What Is the NCAA?

The National Collegiate Athletic Association (NCAA) is the governing body for virtually all college football. Member schools join one of three divisions:

- Division III schools are usually small and do not formally offer athletic scholarships. In Division III, athletics are viewed as merely extracurricular activities, not as a way for the school to make money.
- Division II schools offer athletic scholarships, though they have a limited number to offer. These programs generally do not have the enormous money or fan support necessary to participate in Division I, but they nevertheless offer competitive teams.
- Division I is the most competitive level of NCAA football. Teams have large stadiums, and many fans come to watch every game. They offer large numbers of athletic scholarships. The schools make lots and lots of money from selling tickets, merchandise, and television rights.

Division I has two subdivisions:

- The Championship Subdivision used to be called Division I-AA. These are the smaller schools, which attract fewer than 15,000 fans on average to their games. At the end of the year, sixteen teams enter a playoff to determine a champion.
- The Football Bowl Subdivision used to be called Division 1-A. These are the football powers that want to contend for a national championship. Virtually all of the teams you see on TV are from this subdivision. For many years, the Football Bowl Subdivision had no playoff. From 1998 until 2013, a single two-team playoff game determined the national champion. Since 2014, a four-team playoff has been used to crown a champion.

College Football Compared to NFL Football

You might not notice the different kinds of players, the different schedules, the different rules of college football. Here's a quick summary.

Who Plays?

The most important difference is also the most obvious: College football players are actual college students who live on campus, go to class, and can graduate from the school after several years. They still participate in college life in many of the same ways that physics majors do, and some of them may even be physics majors. College football players are not formally paid, though some of them are given a full scholarship. This means they don't have to pay for tuition, housing, food, or other typical living expenses. However, college football players are not allowed to earn money for autographs, commercials, or anything else associated with their fame as football players.

A college football player is only allowed to play for his team for four years while he is a student. Since it takes most students a while to develop their skills and their bodies to the necessary level, most players are starters for only one or two years. Fans get used to watching new players each year.

A Shorter Schedule

The college schedule is shorter than the NFL schedule. Play starts in late August, when most of the really good teams play weaker teams in order to start the season with some wins. Conference play begins by late September. After twelve games, the regular season schedule is complete by late November. Some conferences hold a championship game in early December, while the lower divisions hold national playoffs. Football Bowl Subdivision teams who win at least six games can be invited to play in bowl games, which usually happen in late December or early January.

Super Sized

Use the picture and letter equations to spell out the silly answer to this riddle.

What kind of football player wears the biggest helmet?

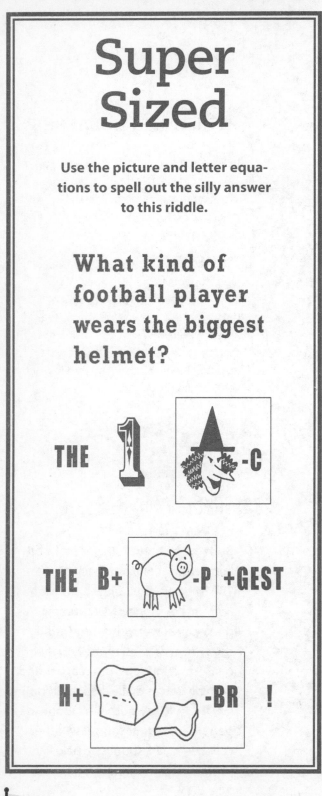

Different Rules

College football is just about the same game that the NFL plays. There are a few minor differences that you'll only notice if you watch carefully. For example, college teams get the ball on the 3-yard line to try for an extra point; NFL teams get the ball on the 2-yard line. The hash marks, where the ball is put in play, are farther apart in college. The NFL requires a receiver to get both his feet in bounds to catch the ball fairly; college receivers only need one foot down. Both levels play for four fifteen-minute quarters, but they have different rules about when the clock stops and when it runs. As a result, college games usually take longer to play than pro games.

Perhaps the biggest difference between pro and college football is the overtime procedure. In the NFL, overtime is played just like the rest of the game, but (with minor exceptions) the team that scores first wins. In college, one team gets the ball at the other team's 25-yard line and tries to score. Then, the other team gets the ball at the same spot. Whoever scores more points wins. If the teams are still tied, they go again until one team comes out of overtime with more points than the other.

The Fans

NFL teams represent a city. People become fans if they grew up near the team. NCAA teams represent their school as well as their community. Most of the student body has some connection to the football team. Some students are band members or cheerleaders, and student managers help the coaches run drills. Students who aren't directly involved with the

team might at least know someone on campus who is involved—maybe they're in a class with the star quarterback or they use the fitness center at the same time as the cheerleading squad. Students usually get cheap tickets and dress in school colors ready to make noise in the crowd.

Because football is such an important part of their social life during college, people who go to colleges with football teams tend to develop a lifelong love for their team. Colleges have alumni clubs, in which graduates pay money to get special seating at games, meetings with coaches, and parties at the stadium with their friends. Graduates bring their own children to games, building loyalty throughout families.

But not all fans are students and alumni. A college team draws fans from the surrounding community. Especially when there's no NFL team nearby, college football becomes the biggest event on Saturday and throughout the year. For example, most of the state of Nebraska is a long day's drive from Denver, where

Football GREAT

Red Grange
The Galloping Ghost first became nationally famous while he played for the University of Illinois. In a 1924 game at Michigan, he scored five touchdowns, four of which came in the first quarter. Red joined the Chicago Bears after graduation, where he earned the then-unimaginable salary of $100,000 for the season.

Conferences for Other Sports

Most teams play in the same conference for all sports, not just football. For example, in the 2006 football season, the University of Florida Gators won the SEC. In March 2007, the Gators also won the SEC basketball tournament.

Conference Names

The Pac-12 includes, as you might expect, twelve teams from the Pacific Coast. But don't be fooled: The Big Ten conference for years had eleven teams, and now has fourteen. The Big 12 conference used to be called the Big 8, but now has . . . ten teams. Go figure.

the closest NFL team plays. But they're not concerned. To them, it is the University of Nebraska Cornhuskers games on Saturdays that they care most about. Los Angeles, California, didn't have a team since the Rams and Raiders left in the late twentieth century. So the two biggest college teams, the UCLA Bruins and the USC Trojans, became the true hometown favorites.

How College Football Is Organized: Conferences

More than 100 teams make up the Football Bowl Subdivision of NCAA Division I. Teams play only twelve regular season games each year, so there's no way that a team can play every other team. A conference consists of eight to twelve teams from one region of the country and usually includes schools of similar size and stature. Each team plays most of the other teams in its conference every year.

Teams join conferences for many reasons. Most important is for money: Conferences have rules to ensure that every team makes some money each year. For example, if a team plays in a bowl game, some of the money they make is distributed among all the teams in the conference. This way, a team makes money even in years when it isn't doing well. Another reason for being part of a conference is for the schedule. Since about eight of every year's games are conference games, the school only has to look for three or four other games to schedule. Of those eight or so conference games, usually four are guaranteed to be home games. Without a conference, it might be difficult to find teams to play, especially teams that are willing to play as a visiting team.

NCAA Football Bowl Subdivision Conferences

The five best-known and most important conferences are:

- **The Southeastern Conference (SEC):** Schools in this conference come from as far north as Kentucky and as far west as Texas. The most recent expansion in 2012 brought the league up to 14 teams with the addition of Texas A&M and Missouri. In recent years, Alabama, Auburn, and Louisiana State have made it to the national championship game. In fact, every national champion from 2006 to 2012 was from the SEC.

- **The Big Ten:** You might think that a conference called the Big Ten would include ten teams, but it actually contains fourteen schools. Why? The Big Ten had only ten teams from 1950 until 1990, but since then has added Penn State, Nebraska, Maryland, and Rutgers. While Ohio State and Michigan have by far won more Big Ten championships than anyone else, Wisconsin and Michigan State have won the league in six of the last seven years.

- **The Pac-12:** Formerly the Pacific Coast Conference, this conference includes twelve teams from the western part of the country after adding Colorado and Utah in 2011. The University of Southern California Trojans dominated the Pac-12 through most of the 2000s, finishing at the top of the standings from 2002–2008. USC has won 36 conference titles, far more than anyone else. However, Stanford and Oregon have won every title since 2009.

- **The Atlantic Coast Conference (ACC):** The ACC is still better known as a power basketball conference than a football conference. Historically great basketball programs from North Carolina, Duke, Wake Forest, North Carolina State, and the rest of the conference have often taken the spotlight away from football. In the 1990s and 2000s, the

The World's Biggest Mascot

At the beginning of every half, the Pac-12 Colorado Buffaloes are led onto the football field by Ralphie, a live buffalo.

The World's Cutest Mascot

The mascot of the Northern Illinois Huskies is a husky—a real, live Siberian husky dog named Mission. He is trained to give cheerleaders high-fives when Northern Illinois scores.

league added several "football schools," including Miami, Florida State, and Boston College. Now the ACC has 14 teams, not all of which are located near the Atlantic Coast. Clemson and Florida State have each won 15 ACC championships, including every title since 2011.

- **The Big 12:** Despite the name, the Big 12 only includes ten teams. In the early 2010s, four famous football schools left the conference and were replaced by Texas Christian University and the University of West Virginia. Though Texas is perhaps the most famous school in the Big 12, Oklahoma has won nine conference titles since 2000.

The five conferences just described generally command the best players and the most television and fan attention. Some of the conferences even have their own TV networks! The other Football Bowl Subdivision conferences have strong programs that are competitive with each other, but they usually have a hard time when facing power conference teams. In fact, a bigger program will often pay a smaller team a lot of money to play a game at the bigger school's home field. Why? The big team gets a home game that they're likely to win. The smaller team may not like the idea of getting crushed in a road game, but the money they make might pay for a large number of scholarships or a new fitness center. And who knows? A few times every year, a school from a not-power conference beats a bigtime team. In 2013, for example, the mighty Florida Gators of the SEC lost to the Georgia Southern Eagles of the Sun Belt Conference.

Determining a National Champion

A four-team tournament determines the national champion. A selection committee made up of 13 members evaluates and ranks the top 25 teams. They begin publishing their rankings in October, though those midseason rankings are meaningless. The top four teams in the final rankings after the conference championship games determine the participants in the College Football Playoff. The semifinals are played on New

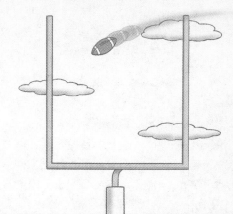

TABLE 4-1: National Champions

1996	Florida Gators
1997	Michigan Wolverines and Nebraska Cornhuskers
1998	Tennessee Volunteers
1999	Florida State Seminoles
2000	Oklahoma Sooners
2001	Miami Hurricanes
2002	Ohio State Buckeyes
2003	Louisiana State Tigers and Southern California Trojans
2004	Southern California Trojans
2005	Texas Longhorns
2006	Florida Gators
2007	Louisiana State Tigers
2008	Florida Gators
2009	Alabama Crimson Tide
2010	Auburn Tigers
2011	Alabama Crimson Tide
2012	Alabama Crimson Tide
2013	Florida State Seminoles
2014	Ohio State Buckeyes
2015	Alabama Crimson Tide

Cold, Blue Turf?

Bowl games are usually played in warm places like Hawaii, Florida, or California. But the famous Idaho Potato Bowl is played in the very cold city of Boise, Idaho. The field for this bowl game is artificial turf, not natural grass—and the turf is painted blue! Rumor has it that migrating geese sometimes crash into the blue turf because they think it's a lake!

Rivalry Story: The "Kick Six"

In 2013, Auburn and Alabama were tied with only one second remaining. Alabama tried to kick a very long field goal for the win. Auburn's Chris Davis waited in the back of the end zone just in case the field goal came up short, which it did, falling into Davis's hands. Davis returned the missed field goal into the field of play and then up the sideline, where he broke free. Auburn radio announcer Rod Bramblett joyously called out, "Davis is gonna run it all the way back! Auburn is gonna win the football game! Auburn is gonna win the football game!"

Year's Day or New Year's Eve as part of the traditional bowl games. Then, in mid-January, the semifinal winners play a national championship in a major national event. Before 1998, the national champion was determined exclusively by a vote of football reporters and coaches. If the reporters and coaches choose different teams, as they did in 1997, both teams were recognized as national champions.

From 1998 to 2014, the winner of a two-team playoff called the "Bowl Championship Series" was recognized by the NCAA as the national champion. However, occasionally, the final reporters' poll of the year ranked a different team number one. In that case, the national championship was shared by the BCS winner and the number one team in the reporters' poll. This happened in 2003: Louisiana State University won the BCS championship, but the reporters voted Southern Cal as the best team. Both teams are considered to be 2003 national champions.

Bowl Games

Even though only four teams make the College Football Playoff, any team that wins six or more games gets to play in a postseason game called a bowl game. What are these, what do they mean, and why are there so many?

The Way It Was

Before the 1990s, there weren't very many bowl games, and each one was extra special and extra popular. In those days, most people couldn't see more than one or two college football games per week. If you lived, say, in Ohio, you might never have seen a Pac-12 game all year. The bowl games were the fans' opportunity to see some of the great teams they had heard so much about. As for the teams, only the winner of a conference or a few selected other great teams got to play in a bowl. The four New Year's Day bowl games—the Rose

Bowl, Cotton Bowl, Orange Bowl, and Sugar Bowl—were the highlight of the season for the fans.

Bowl Games Today

After the 2015 season, there were 40 bowl games played in the weeks before and the week after New Year's Day. More than half of the Football Bowl Subdivision teams play in a bowl; virtually all power conference teams play in a bowl. Now that most regular season games are on television throughout the country and almost any team can make it to a bowl, bowls are not as big a deal as they used to be. In fact, there are so many bowl games that even teams with losing records are sometimes invited to play.

But they're still fun! Millions of fans still watch the games and the players have a good time. Teams that make it to bowls are allowed extra practice time to prepare. Teams make use of this time not only to get ready for the bowl but also to give younger players experience so they'll be ready to replace the graduating seniors the next year. Most bowls may not be truly special games, but they'll keep being played as long as people keep watching.

The Best College Football Rivalries

Most schools have a single most hated rival, a team they play only once each year but whose game dominates the season. A true rivalry means that, during the first part of the season, fans of both teams actively root against their rival, no matter who they play. A team would rather go 1-10 while beating their rival than go 10-1 with a loss to their rival. Most rivalry games are played the week before Thanksgiving, though some are played Thanksgiving weekend.

Here is a look at the four best-known college football rivalries:

The Stanford Axe

At a Cal-Stanford baseball game in 1899, Cal students stole an axe from the Stanford cheerleaders. Cal kept that axe in a bank vault for thirty-one years, until a crew of Stanford students launched an elaborate and successful plot to steal it back. Now, whichever team wins the Big Game gets to keep the axe for a year. At Stanford pep rallies, cheerleaders still refer to "the Stanford axe that California has wrongly stolen from us, that it is our responsibility to retrieve."

Rivalry Story

Legendary Ohio State coach Woody Hayes hated Michigan—not just the university, but the whole state and anything associated with it. It is said that when the Ohio State team bus was running out of gas on the way home to Ohio, Coach Hayes refused to stop at any gas station in the state of Michigan, even if he might have to walk for miles to get more gas.

Auburn-Alabama

The Iron Bowl matches the two biggest football schools in the state of Alabama. It is said that anyone who moves into Alabama is immediately asked to declare whether they are an Auburn or an Alabama fan. The teams didn't play each other between 1907 and 1947 because the schools couldn't agree on how to get unbiased referees. The Alabama Crimson Tide have won nine more games than the Auburn Tigers in the history of the rivalry.

Stanford-California

The Big Game, as it's known, pits these San Francisco Bay Area schools against each other each year. Both schools are best known for their strong academic programs, and they have produced plenty of NFL players. In the days leading up to the game, the California freshmen chemistry classes all get together for a special demonstration in which the professor turns a red flask blue with just one drop of a chemical. (Red is Stanford's color; blue and gold are California's colors.)

Ohio State-Michigan

These schools have each won seven national championships, and together they have won nearly half of all Big Ten championships in conference history. As a result, the yearly Michigan-Ohio State game often decides the Big Ten champion. There is nothing more important to fans of these schools than beating their rival. Former OSU coach John Cooper won more than 70 percent of his games and three conference championships. But his record against Michigan was 2-10-1, so he was fired in 2000. Since then, Ohio State has won all but two games in this rivalry.

Go Team!

A very visible part of any football team are the cheerleaders! The first organized cheer was during a college football game over 100 years ago, in 1898. Believe it or not, that original cheer is still being used at the University of Minnesota today! Use the decoder to fill in the blanks, and then give this cheer a try—outside the house, of course!

A = ✳
H = ★
I = ☆
N = ☆
O = ☆
S = ✳
Y = ◉

R✳★, R✳★, R✳★!

✳K☆-U-M✳★,

★★☆-R✳★!

★★☆-R✳★!

V✳R✳☆T◉!

V✳R✳☆T◉!

V✳R✳☆T◉,

M☆☆☆★-E-✳☆★-T✳★!

FUN FACT

Bill the Goat

Bill is the Naval Academy mascot. He's a live goat who attends every Army-Navy game. He has been kidnapped several times in history, by cadets at both Air Force and Army, but each time Naval Intelligence tracked him down and obtained his release.

The Commander-in-Chief's Trophy

This coveted award is presented to the team with the best record in the yearly games between Army, Navy, and Air Force. Though Air Force has won the trophy the most times, Navy has won nine of the past eleven years.

Army-Navy

Each branch of the United States armed forces has its own academy. To attend, a student must meet very strict academic and physical requirements. Everyone at the service academies, not just the athletes, gets a full scholarship. All students take challenging courses and receive military training, and they must spend several years in the armed forces when they graduate. Student life is quite different at Army and Navy (and Air Force) than it is at other Division I schools.

It's understandable, then, that the academies aren't usually in the hunt for a national championship. Yet the Army-Navy rivalry is perhaps the most intense in the country. Cadets and Midshipmen arrive at the game in Philadelphia in full uniform. They put on displays of pushups when their team scores. The game is carried on the Armed Forces Network, meaning that everyone in the Army and the Navy, even people who are deployed overseas, can watch the game on television or listen to it over the radio. The game has always been an important television event in the United States. In fact, the first time that a replay was ever shown during a televised football game was during an Army-Navy game.

College Football Beyond Division I

Every year, thousands and thousands of good high school football players graduate and go to college. Only the very best are offered scholarships for Division I teams. Though the majority of these high school graduates will never make it to the NFL, they might not be ready to end their football careers. One option for them is to play football at a Division II or a Division III school.

Lower-division colleges don't have 100,000-seat stadiums and national television cameras at the games. At the same time, their games are usually much bigger events than high school games, with large stadiums, big crowds, and a high quality of play. Fans of lower-division football teams point out that going to their games can be a better experience than going to a big school's games because admission is cheaper, the stadium is less cramped, and there's no need to fight for a parking space.

Perhaps the most fun aspect of Division II and III football is the national championship playoff at the end of the season. The very best teams get to host as many as three playoff games at home. The national final in each division is shown on national television. The Division II championship is played at the University of North Alabama every year. Colorado

What's in a Name?

All college teams have some kind of nickname. Frequently, animals are used for both the nickname and the team mascot. Break the Letter Switch code (B=A, C=B, D=C, etc.) to learn the four most popular animal nicknames!

Some teams choose more unusual nicknames. Break the Vowel Switch code to learn some of these lesser known mascots!

FBHMFT   CVMMEPHT   UJHFST   MJPOT

PUNGIANS   KONGOREUS   EWLS   BLIU HUNS

FUN FACT

Eddie Robinson

In 1941, Grambling State University, a Division I-AA college in northern Louisiana, hired coach Eddie Robinson. Until 1997 (that's fifty-six years!), Robinson coached the Tigers to 408 victories, the second most ever for a coach in Division I. More than 200 of his players entered the NFL. That would be a lot for a huge Division I program, let alone for a coach in a lower division.

State-Pueblo won in 2014; Northwest Missouri State won in both 2013 and 2015.

In Division III, the championship game is called the Amos Alonzo Stagg Bowl, named after the famous coach of the University of Chicago's football team from the early 1900s. The Stagg Bowl is played each year in Salem, Virginia. Either Wisconsin–Whitewater or Mount Union has won every Division III championship since 2005.

TRY THIS

Beyond Football

If you want to become a better football player, try playing a different sport during the offseason. Any competitive activity will keep your body in shape and help you improve your athletic skills. Anything that encourages competition, mental toughness, and a winning attitude will help when football season arrives.

There's a Team for Everyone

The pros take center stage on Sundays, and college football seems to dominate fall Saturdays in America. But Friday nights belong to the high schools. Most high schools, public and private, sponsor a football team. Since most teenagers attend high schools within their local area, high school teams truly represent communities. You have probably met some of the players on the nearby high school team, and you might even have relatives on a team. Perhaps you'd like to play high school football one day.

Varsity, Junior Varsity, and Freshman Teams

The team that represents the school on Friday night includes the best players in the school, and it is called the varsity team. The majority of varsity players are juniors and seniors. Unless a younger player is unusually fast or way bigger than normal for his age, he's probably not ready to play varsity.

Depending on the size of the school, there might be other teams to join. The junior varsity (JV) team often includes players who are not quite good enough to play regularly on the varsity, or perhaps players who are good enough to play varsity but who are still too young or too small to start. The JV team might play on Monday instead of Friday or might play a Friday afternoon game right before the varsity game. If the school is big enough, it might sponsor a third team, one just for freshmen. The lower-level teams give you a good way to play the game, have fun, and develop your skills. The best way to become good enough for the varsity team is to play hard and to play well at the freshman and JV level.

The Offseason—Getting in Shape

The game of football requires enormous physical effort, and it can give your body a bit of a beating. You must be

Twin Teammates

There are ten differences between the uniforms and equipment shown here. Can you find them?

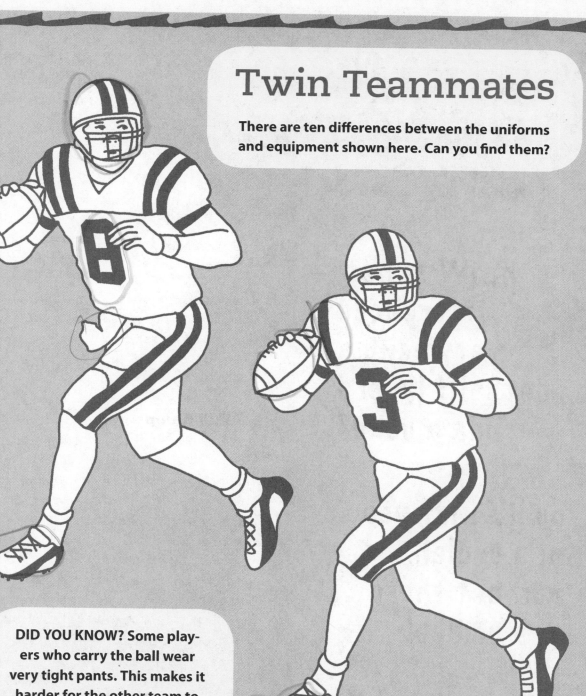

DID YOU KNOW? Some players who carry the ball wear very tight pants. This makes it harder for the other team to grab their pants to stop them!

in good shape to play any kind of football, and the higher the level of your game, the more speed, strength, endurance, and flexibility you must develop. A high school football player cannot spend all summer just lying on the beach and playing video games. Someone who does so will likely not make it through the first practice, let alone any games.

A high school coach will usually give the players a summer workout program that will gradually build up the players' fitness. The idea is to come into preseason practices ready to play hard. Offseason workouts include lots of running and weightlifting. The team might come in all together a couple of times per week for their workouts. Players who go on long vacations or who do special summer trips can still run, do pushups and sit-ups, and find a place to do weightlifting occasionally.

Skill Camps

The summer is the time when many colleges offer camps to help players develop their skills. These may last a couple of days or as long as a week. The college's coaching staff often runs these camps. They show the players drills, films, and conditioning exercises that will help them develop into better players. The camps can be a chance to compete against and practice with top players from other schools. By the end of the camp, everyone has a pretty good idea of what he can do well, which skills still need improvement, and who the really, really good players are.

A great way for a team to improve together over the summer is to play in a 7-on-7 league or to attend a 7-on-7 camp. Sure, it's important to develop individual skills, but it's even more crucial to play with your teammates in competitive situations. In a 7-on-7 game, quarterbacks can practice reading coverages and can learn how their receivers will react to different defenses. Defensive backs can practice not just one-on-one defense, but can be part of an entire coverage scheme. If you're playing a game, then what you're doing feels like more than just practice. A great play can actually score a touchdown, just as in a real football game, and a mistake may cost points. The team is practicing under nearly real game conditions. When the team is faced with a truly real game in the fall, they will know how to react. They will have confidence in their teammates and in themselves, hopefully leading to a few extra wins.

Right Before the Season

The team gets together for two weeks or so of preseason practice. The coaching staff usually has two goals for this time:

- Teach the team how plays are called and what to do on each play.
- Improve players' techniques so everyone becomes a better player at his position.

To accomplish these goals, many different teaching tools might be used. For example, the team might have classroom meetings with a chalkboard and notebooks to explain how some plays are supposed to work. On another day, the team might watch video of a college team executing these plays successfully. Sometimes it's useful to watch video of yesterday's practice to show who ran the plays correctly or incorrectly.

On the field, a chunk of practice is devoted to skill development with the position coaches. During this time, the players run drills that help them practice a technique. For example, quarterbacks may work on hitting a target or on reading the safeties and throwing

What Is 7-on-7?

In a 7-on-7 drill, the offensive and defensive lines are removed so the team can focus just on the passing game. The defense plays with three linebackers and four defensive backs; the offense gets a center, five running backs or receivers, and a quarterback.

The Tip Drill

One of the defenders' favorite drills is called the tip drill. In one version, the coach throws a pass to a running receiver, who deliberately misses the catch and tips the ball in the air. The defenders have to catch the ball for an interception. If they can't catch the ball cleanly, they're taught to try to keep the ball in the air. Defenses love interceptions, and they can make an interception on every play of this drill.

Football GREAT

Reggie White
Reggie, a defensive end nick-named the Minister of Defense, lived all of his early life in Chattanooga, Tennessee. He went to the Howard School of Academics and Technology for high school and the University of Tennessee for college. His NFL career included dominant years with both the Philadelphia Eagles and the Green Bay Packers.

away from them. Linebackers may repeatedly practice taking a read step and dropping into coverage.

Another big chunk of preseason practice time is devoted to rehearsing plays. The offense might start by running the plays on air, meaning that they just go through what they're supposed to do without any defense around. Next, a few managers or second-string players might hold pads and stand where defenders might be. Eventually, the offense knows the plays well enough to run them against a live defense.

Scouting the Opponent

Once the season starts, both the offense and the defense usually know all of the team's plays. The question then becomes which of these plays will work best against the next opponent. Figuring out which plays to use is called scouting, and it is one of the coaching staff's biggest jobs.

Well before each game, teams trade tapes. They send video of their old games to their next opponent. The weekend before a game, the coaching staff watches this tape carefully. First, they figure out who the opponent's best players are and which are the best units. They'll also try to find the other team's weak spots. Perhaps their cornerbacks look really good, but their defensive linemen seem to get pushed back on every play. Then they decide what strategy to use to beat this team. Perhaps on offense they need to use a power running game, mixed with a few deep passes if the safeties come up to stop the run. Whatever they decide, the coaching staff must have a clear plan ready before Monday's practice: that's when they start preparing the team for the game.

The Week Before a Game

Practice during the season runs a bit differently from preseason practices. Much less time is set aside to work on skills and techniques because more time is necessary to establish and practice the week's game plan.

The Scout Team

Most football teams include a good number of players who don't get much playing time in games. These folks aren't the starters, and sometimes they aren't even the backups for the starters. But they can play an essential role in practice.

Once the coaching staff has scouted the upcoming opponent, they know how that opponent plays: what formations they use on offense, which kinds of plays they run, and what strategies they use on defense. To prepare for this opponent, the coaching staff chooses a scout team made up of nonstarters. The scout team pretends to be the upcoming opponent. Their job is to give the starters practice seeing the same kind of football team that they will see on Friday night. If enough players are available, two scout teams could be formed—one for offense, one for defense.

Early in the week, the coaches explain the game plan and practice the specific plays or defenses that will be used. First the offense and defense practice separately, making sure they know what to do. Toward the end of practice, the offense and defense will run against the scout team. The coaching staff can tell which of their ideas will work (and which won't) by noticing how the scout team does. If the scout team is stopping the offense, then the offense probably needs a new game plan.

By the end of the week, the players all know what to do. Practice might then consist of special game situations, like trying to score from the 2-yard line or stopping the offense on third down and long. Maybe the team will even play a ghost game, in which the starters and the scout team play a shortened version of a real game, complete with a coin toss, kickoffs, and coaches pretending to be referees.

FUN FACT

Impersonating Star Players

If the next opponent has a really good player, the scout team might assign their best athlete to pretend to be that star. On some teams, the star player on the scout team gets to wear a special jersey with the number of the opposing player. Being chosen to impersonate the opponent's best player is a big deal for a scout team player.

WORDS to KNOW

HOMECOMING: One home game each fall is the homecoming game. That's when students who already graduated come back to the school to see each other and show their support for their former high school. Homecoming events include more than just a football game—usually there's also a parade, a dance, and maybe even other events.

Boarding School Football

There are options for high school beyond local public and private schools. At boarding school, you live with the faculty and other students. Usually, boarding school students are required to participate in sports, and joining football teams can be wonderful experiences for the players. There are all kinds of boarding schools with football teams. Fork Union Military Academy in Virginia offers "cadets" leadership and military training. Their football team is almost always in the state playoffs. Christian Hackenberg, Penn State's quarterback, attended Fork Union. Woodberry Forest School's atmosphere is like that of a liberal arts college; their players are also in musicals or on the physics team. Woodberry has been state champion most years since the late 2000s. Notre Dame running back C.J. Prosise attended Woodberry. Boarding school games offer a different atmosphere than typical high school games. Games are often played on Saturday afternoon rather than Friday night. The players are from all over, so there's not usually a crowd of local supporters, but the student section is often enthusiastic. Many schools broadcast their games over the Internet so that the far-away parents and alumni can follow along.

Thursday's practice before a Friday night game is usually a relaxed practice. The players are storing up their energy for the next day's game. They don't want to get banged up or sore without time to recover. But the players can still run through their plays, and they generally go through the motions of beating the opponent. By the end of Thursday's practice, the team will be ready for the game.

State Championships

High school teams play eight to eleven regular season games. Just like college teams are members of a conference, high school teams play many of their games against the same schools every year. In high school, this group of schools is usually called a district, though the term is different in some states. The regular season schedule usually includes one game against each of the other teams in the same district. Districts are chosen to include similar-sized schools from the same local area.

At season's end, the best team or teams in the district advance to the state playoffs. Though big and small schools might play regular season games against each other, in the playoffs, teams only play schools of about the same size. The state association sets up tournaments similar to the college Division II and Division III playoffs. The winner of each playoff game advances to the next round. Eventually, the remaining teams are from different parts of the state. The championship games—one in each size category—are often held in a major college or NFL stadium because of the huge crowds that show up.

Chapter 6

OFFENSIVE FOOTBALL

Stars 21
Wolves 14

Pep Rally

If there's a big football game that night, students will be thinking about their team all day at school. Use the clues to help complete these words that are full of team spirit!

lunch wrappers and empty lunch bag

_ R A _ H

mistake in Drivers' Ed.

_ R A _ H

important to have in chorus

_ _ A _ H

art project with dried flowers

_ _ R A _ H

what boring teachers do

_ _ R A _ H

activity in math class

_ R A _ H

after-school fundraiser

_ _ R A _ H

What Is the Offense?

The offense is the unit on a football team that tries to carry the ball into the end zone. They can use all sorts of different plays and strategies to move the ball. At its heart, though, every play is either a running play or a passing play.

Running Plays

On running plays, the quarterback usually hands the ball to a running back. Sometimes the quarterback will keep the ball and run it himself. Either way, on running plays the offensive line tries to push the defensive team back in order to give the runner holes to run through. Running plays will usually gain a few yards. It's unlikely that a team will lose yards running the ball, but it's also unlikely that they'll make big gains. Running is especially important for a team that is trying to hold on to a lead because the clock will almost always keep counting down after a running play.

Passing Plays

On passing plays, the quarterback holds the ball and tries to throw it to one of his receivers. The offensive line doesn't push down the field; rather, it drops back and tries to keep the defensive team away from the quarterback. Passing plays are riskier than running plays—passes can be intercepted, and the offense doesn't gain any yards if a pass isn't caught. But passes are also the way to make big gains.

A good offense is balanced and includes both passing and running plays. Sure, some teams use one type of play more than the other, depending on their players' strengths. But every team must be able to both pass and run.

The precise design of passing and running plays has changed a lot over the past century. Today, teams use all sorts of offensive schemes. A later section of this chapter explains some of the possible strategies that an offense can use. All successful offenses use the same basic types of players: a clever quarterback, a strong offensive line, and powerful or fast receivers and running backs. The first part of this chapter will explain the jobs of each type of player.

Joe Montana as . . . the Quarterback

The quarterback is the boss on the field. At the start of pretty much every play, the quarterback gets the ball, and he starts the action. Different offensive schemes may require the quarterback to do different things with the ball. For example, an option-based offense might have the quarterback run the ball (or at least pretend to run the ball) on every play. Most NFL offenses have the quarterback drop back five to seven steps on every play, each time either handing the ball to a running back or passing from the pocket.

Adjusting the Play

During a football game, the coach usually tells the quarterback what kind of play to run. But once the teams have lined up, the quarterback has to decide whether that play is likely to work. For example, imagine that the coach calls a running play to the right side. The quarterback should notice how the defense lines up. If the defense has a lot of players waiting on the right, where the running back is supposed to go, then the quarterback should make the decision to change the play.

One way to change a play is to use code words. Right before the snap, you'll see the quarterback shouting signals to his team. Often, those signals don't mean

WORDS to KNOW

POCKET: When the quarterback has dropped back to pass, his offensive line forms a horseshoe-shaped pocket around him. They push the pass rushers toward the sideline and down the field, keeping the area around the quarterback clear of defenders until the quarterback can throw a pass.

······ Football ······ GREAT

Joe Montana

Joe Cool, as he became known, started his career with the San Francisco 49ers in 1979. In only his third year, he led the 49ers to their best NFL season ever: a 13-3 record and a playoff berth. Joe was named the most valuable player in three of his four Super Bowl victories. Throughout his career, Joe was known for his grace under pressure. Twenty-six times he led the 49ers to come-from-behind wins. That's where the nickname Joe Cool came from. Even when his team trailed, they believed Joe could lead them back.

The Silly Answer Is "The One in the Sugar Bowl!"

What's the silly question? To find out, use the directions to cross words out of the grid. Read the remaining words from left to right and top to bottom!

..........................Cross out............................

...sports that use nets   ...places to keep clothes
...two-letter words without I   ...insects that don't fly

IF	TENNIS	TWO	ANTS
ON	FLIES	ARE	BASKETBALL
EARWIGS	CLOSET	AN	FLEAS
IN	VOLLYBALL	THE	DRESSER
SPIDERS	KITCHEN	HAMPER	WHICH
AT	ONE	ROACHES	UP
IS	OR	THE	PING-PONG
BADMINTON	FOOTBALL	OF	PLAYER

anything. But everyone on the team knows a few special words for plays. When the quarterback uses those code words, then everyone knows to ignore the play the coach called and instead to run a new play. The code words the quarterback uses are called audibles.

Sometimes the quarterback has options to avoid a stacked defense even after the play starts. The simplest example is that the quarterback might choose to keep the ball and run the other way if a running back is about to run into a blitzing linebacker. A more complicated example is that if he sees a blitz coming, the quarterback can throw to the "hot" receiver.

Two Dominant Quarterbacks

Peyton Manning joined the Indianapolis Colts in 1998 after starting for four years at the University of Tennessee. His Colts only won three games in his first year. But for the next twelve years, the Colts under Manning went to the playoffs eleven times and won the Super Bowl after the 2006 season.

Unlike most quarterbacks, who mainly run the plays their coaches call, Manning controlled his offense himself. Before each snap, the coach suggested a few plays, and Manning chose from those or called one of his own.

He was a master at game strategy, reacting to anything the defense tried to do. At the line of scrimmage, Manning was known for flapping his arms like a chicken, squawking out real and fake signals in order to tell his teammates what play to run.

How did he always know what his offense should do? Manning was one of the best-prepared football players in the NFL. He watched tape for hours, picking out defensive formations and defensive players he could take advantage of. He practiced with his team but also privately with his receivers. Thanks to an excellent coaching staff and Peyton's attention to detail, the whole Broncos offense was able to adjust their game plan moment by moment in a game.

WORDS to KNOW

HOT RECEIVER: A blitz is when lots of unexpected defenders rush toward the quarterback. The quarterback has to get rid of the ball quickly! On many passing plays, one receiver runs a very short route, called a hot route, and gets ready to catch the ball right away. If the quarterback sees a blitz, he knows he can throw right away to the hot receiver to avoid being sacked.

Brady-Manning Rivalry

Tom Brady's first NFL start was a victory against Peyton Manning and the Colts in 2001. It was the beginning of an intense rivalry. Manning did not find a way to beat Brady's Patriots until 2005. The two faced off against each other seventeen times, the last five while Manning was with the Broncos. Brady ended up with eleven wins to Manning's six.

Anthony Muñoz

As a kid, Anthony Muñoz was too big to play Pop Warner football. He was even big for the NFL when the Cincinnati Bengals drafted him in 1980. He was named an All-Pro eleven times in thirteen seasons with the Bengals. Anthony could move quickly, allowing him to get in front of any defensive lineman. His workout routine was intense, involving not just weightlifting but also running, sprinting, and agility drills.

Manning battled injuries in the 2010s as he aged into his late 30s. He left the Colts to sign with the Denver Broncos in 2012, taking his new team to the playoffs five years in a row as well as to two Super Bowls and an NFL championship. Manning set the NFL single-season record with 55 touchdown passes in 2013. Manning retired in 2016 after bringing the Broncos to victory in Super Bowl 50.

Tom Brady was an extremely accomplished college quarterback. However, he was not drafted in the first round of the NFL draft in 2000. Nope, 198 players were chosen before he was. Most of those teams who passed on him now regret their decision, as Brady has had tremendous success with the New England Patriots. In fourteen full seasons as a starter, he led his team to six Super Bowls, winning four of them (and earning the MVP trophy in three of them). His teams have always won more than they lost; he's won nearly 80 percent of the games he's started, including an undefeated 16-0 regular season in 2007.

Brady is best known for his playoff successes. Like his idol Joe Montana, Tom has repeatedly authored game-winning drives in crucial games. He holds the record for the most consecutive wins of any quarterback in the postseason with ten. He is just as good or better under the intense pressure of a playoff game as he is in the first game of the season.

Anthony Muñoz Anchors . . . the Offensive Line

A team's offensive linemen are the men who move mountains. They have one job: to block the defense. On running plays, they open up lanes for running backs to run through. On passing plays, they protect the quarterback by forming a pocket. It takes a special kind of unselfish person to be an offensive lineman. Fans rarely hear about the linemen, except when they are called for a penalty. Linemen don't usually score touchdowns, don't make tackles, and don't gain yards. Yet the line is the most important unit on the offense. A good offensive line can make a bad running back look great. By giving him time to throw, a good offensive line can make any quarterback who can throw look awesome.

The offensive line consists of the center, who snaps the ball; the two guards, who line up just right and left of the center; and the two offensive tackles, who line up just right and left of the guards.

Running Plays

The first job of the offensive line on a running play is to create a surge. The offensive linemen have an advantage over the defense because they know when the ball will be snapped. When the ball is snapped, the linemen move powerfully in the direction of the play, trying to take two steps before they contact a defender. This process is called firing off the line.

Zone Blocking

Before the snap, all the linemen have to know their responsibilities. They have to know which direction to fire off the line, and they have to know if there's a specific defensive player they're assigned to block.

In zone blocking, the linemen all fire out together in one direction. They block anyone in their way, pushing whichever defender they see. Zone blockers are like trains on a track, knocking down everything in their path and not letting anyone cross. A zone blocker's first responsibility is to block defensive linemen. If no defensive lineman is in the way, the offensive lineman can get to the next level; that is, he can race upfield and block a linebacker. One

WORDS to KNOW

SNAP COUNT: Every play starts when the center snaps the ball to the quarterback. But how does the center know when to snap? The quarterback shouts "Hut!" when he wants the ball. Sometimes, though, the quarterback will shout "Hut, hut!" or even "Hut, hut, hut!" Before every play, the quarterback tells the offense how many times he'll say "Hut" before the snap.

Can You Find the Traps and Pulls?

Now that you know a bit about how linemen play, you can look closely for a pulling guard or a trapping tackle. Each time you notice one of these plays, write down what you saw, whether the lineman made the block he was supposed to make, and how many yards the play gained.

advantage of zone blocking is that no specific offensive player is assigned to get to the next level. Instead, whichever lineman doesn't have anyone to block can be used effectively.

Traps and Pulls

If linemen blocked the same way on every play, the defense would know exactly how to avoid them to make tackles. Traps and pulls are ways for the offense to change strategy to surprise the defense. Guards are usually assigned to trap and pull, but tackles and the center can run these plays just as well.

Imagine a defensive lineman is very fast, so fast that he sometimes beats the offensive player assigned to block him. What can the offense do? Let him get past the offensive line surge. Let the defender think he's going to make a play, but send the tackle from the other side of the field to run behind the line right toward where the defender will be. This tackle blocks the defender sideways and out of the play. Such a play is called a trap because the defender is usually surprised and can't see the tackle coming.

Another way to trick the defense is to pull a guard or tackle into a hole. When the offensive line creates a hole for a running back to run through, the defensive linebackers are coached to get in that hole to stop the running back. To trick the defense, the offense sends the guard from the other side of the field to run into the hole ahead of the running back. The guard blocks the linebacker who thinks he's going to make a play, and the running back can keep running.

Pass Protection

Passing plays are a bit simpler for linemen. Instead of creating a surge, their job is to keep the defenders away from the quarterback. They form a pocket by pushing the rushers forward and to the side. Sometimes the linemen have to stand their ground against a big, strong,

Hide the Football

There are ten football words hiding in these sentences. Can you find them all? We've given you a list of words to look for, but watch out—there are extra words in the list!

BLOCK	*FOULS*	*LINE*	*PUNT*	*SNAP*
CANTER	*FUMBLE*	*PIGSKIN*	*RUSH*	*SWEEP*
CLOCK	*KICK*	*PLAY*	*SCORE*	*TEAM*

1. Is the game on one disc or eleven cassettes?

2. We won! Hear us "Hooray!"

3. The champ lay winded in the end zone.

4. The quarterback spun, then threw the ball.

5. Tired players nap before a big game.

6. Don't panic! Lock the stadium door!

7. All I need is to move the ball four more yards!

8. Losing teams weep in private.

9. All of Ray Spigs' kin came to watch him play!

10. Drinking iced tea makes players less thirsty.

bull-rushing defensive lineman. Sometimes, though, it's good enough just to make the defender go away from the quarterback. On passing plays, all that matters is that the quarterback has enough time to throw. Whether defenders are knocked down or merely pushed aside is not important.

The major difficulty in pass protection is picking up a blitz. When the defense sends five or six players, the quarterback is supposed to notice this and throw to the hot receiver. The line still has to give him enough time to make that throw. It's usually most important to block the players coming up the middle, because they can get to the quarterback fastest. A tackle who sees a blitz might have to leave his man to help out the guard and center. Often, the running back is assigned to help out the offensive line on a blitz—he can block the outside guy that the tackle let go.

Big Excitement: The Tackle-Eligible Play

Once in a long while, a strange formation can put an offensive tackle on the end of the line of scrimmage. Then, the tackle is an eligible receiver for that play. The tackle can pretend to block, then run out for a pass. Especially if this is done near the end zone, the defense can be taken completely by surprise. A quick pass to the wide-open tackle can score an easy touchdown. The tackle-eligible play is very rare. Even Anthony Muñoz only scored four touchdowns in his whole career.

If you plan on playing offensive line for your high school, don't get your hopes up of catching a pass on a tackle-eligible play. The play is illegal under high school rules. You'll have to make it to the NFL to catch a pass as a lineman.

In the NFL Today

Tackle Andrew Whitworth is a key member of the Cincinnati Bengals' offensive line. He played his college football at Louisiana State, where he started 52 games in four years. The Bengals chose him in the second round of the 2006 draft. He began his career as a guard, but he moved to left tackle in 2009. As left tackle, he protects quarterback Andy Dalton's blind side. Whitworth is generally assigned to block the opponent's most fearsome pass rusher on each of 50 or so snaps in a game. While it's easy to look at a running back's yards or a receiver's touchdowns to estimate how good he is, it's difficult to use statistics to say quickly how good an offensive line is. We do know that the Bengals' offensive line finished in the top half of the league in "adjusted line yards" every year since 2011. Beyond that, we have to rely on people's opinions of his work. He was voted second-team All-Pro in 2010 and 2014; he made the Pro Bowl in 2012 and 2015. And, although it had nothing to do with his actual job as an offensive tackle, Whitworth scored a touchdown on a tackle-eligible play in 2010.

Walter Payton Embodies . . . the Running Back

It may seem obvious, but the running back's job is to take a handoff from the quarterback and run. Yes, you knew that already, right? The running back has other jobs as well, but by far the most important is to carry the ball.

A good ballcarrier is not only fast but is also quick and able to change directions on the spur of the moment. Strong running backs can make correct decisions about where to run the ball. When the offensive line is zone blocking, it's not clear right away exactly where the best spot to run will be. The running back has to read his blocks. For example, a zone running play might be designed to get the ball outside, toward the sideline. But if the outside defender has pushed outside to stop this play, the running back has to recognize right

Football GREAT

Walter Payton
Walter "Sweetness" Payton played for thirteen years, from 1975–1987. In 1975, the Bears drafted him with their first pick. Walter set eight NFL records in his career, including the most rushing yards in a single game, most career rushing yards, and most career total yards. Walter Payton remains perhaps the most loved Bear in recent history.

WORDS to KNOW

BALL SECURITY: All of the great running in the world is useless if the running back fumbles the ball. Defenders not only try to tackle the ballcarrier, they also try to take the ball away. By carrying the ball properly and covering the ball with two hands when he's about to be hit, the running back can protect his team's possession.

SCREEN PASS: When the offensive line forms a pocket and the receivers run downfield, the defense is ready for a long pass. Sometimes they forget about the running back. In one common screen pass, the running back and some linemen pretend to miss their blocks so the pass rushers think they can tackle the quarterback. Then the quarterback throws a short pass over the rushers to the running back, who now has a clear field in front of him for a long gain.

away to cut straight up the field or back to the middle, wherever the line has opened up space.

Beyond speed, quickness, and decision-making, the running back has to be tough. The running back probably is tackled more times per game than anyone else. A runner who can still gain a few yards after getting hit by a defender is extremely valuable. If the running back can bounce right up, ready to carry the ball again on the next play, he's making an enormous contribution to the offense.

What else does a running back have to do besides run? First of all, he often has to block on passing plays. Especially if the defense sends a blitz, the running back has to be aware of any rushers that the offensive line might miss.

A Favorite Fantasy Player

A native of Miami, Devonta Freeman won a state championship in high school. He attended Florida State University, where as a junior he rushed for more than 1,000 yards and won the national championship. Freeman then chose to go pro; the Falcons selected him in the third round in 2014. It was more than a year before the Falcons chose to use Freeman as an every-week starter . . . but when they did, he responded with two 3-touchdown games in a row. The fantasy players who chose to draft Freeman in 2015 did very well with him.

Jerry Rice Is . . . the Wide Receiver

The receiver's main job is possibly the simplest to understand: get open, catch the ball, and then run with the ball.

Get Open

On each passing play, a receiver is assigned a route to run. The route tells the receiver which way to run and when to change directions. The receiver and the quarterback will practice that route hundreds of times, so the quarterback will have an idea of when and where to throw the ball. It's the receiver's job to run the route full speed, the same way he ran it in practice, to make it easier for the quarterback to read whether the receiver is open.

Depending on the defense, sometimes a receiver has to adjust the route. For example, it's a bad idea to run right into a defender's zone (an area of the field the defender is responsible for), because then the receiver would be covered easily. Against a zone defense, the receiver might need to stop his route early to stay open. On the other hand, against a man-to-man defense, the receiver should keep running past his defender, or he might need to adjust his route away from his defender.

Catch the Ball

This may sound like an obvious skill not even worthy of mention. But there's nothing more frustrating to an offense than the perfect pass thrown to an open receiver who drops the ball. On the other hand, there's nothing more exciting or inspiring than an outstanding catch. A receiver must work to develop good hands—yes, hands—because the ball should always be caught with the hands, not cradled against the body. Receivers can practice diving for a catch or catching balls that are thrown off target or with a lot of force. The more experience someone has catching difficult passes, the more likely that person is to make the tough catch in the game.

Run!

As soon as the receiver catches the ball, he must tuck the ball away like a running back. Ball security should be first priority. Then he has to get that ball upfield. A receiver who has caught the ball is usually

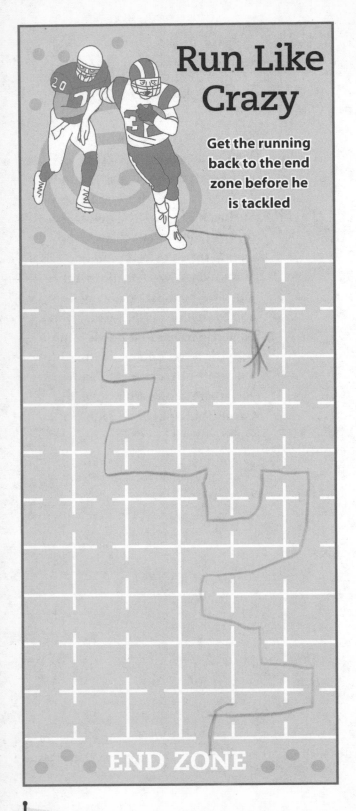

Run Like Crazy

Get the running back to the end zone before he is tackled

END ZONE

far away from the biggest defenders. If he can beat one or two tacklers, he might score a touchdown.

Blocking

Even the best receivers don't get the ball thrown to them more than ten or so times per game. Truly great receivers help their team win on every play.

On running plays, a receiver will usually have a blocking assignment. No, he won't have to block that 320-pound nose tackle, but he might have to block a linebacker or safety so the running back can run toward the sideline. Receivers should learn proper blocking form, especially because they often weigh less than people they're supposed to block. Fortunately, it's not necessary to knock a defender down on every play. Just getting in the way and making some physical contact is often enough. But the stronger a blocker you are, the farther away from you a cornerback might play, letting you take advantage of him on a passing play!

Megatron

Wide receiver Calvin Johnson was a second pick in the 2007 draft. He played for the Detroit Lions for the next decade. Johnson was almost always among the league leaders in receiving yards; in 2012 he set the all-time NFL record for receiving yards in a season. He was a strong, athletic player with outstanding durability: From 2007 to 2015, he played in 135 games and missed only eight. Even though the Lions only had two winning seasons in Johnson's career, and even though opposing teams stacked their defense to try to stop him, Calvin Johnson nevertheless experienced sustained success during his career. He was named to five Pro Bowls, and retired in 2016.

The Receiver Who Makes the Most Catches

No one wanted Wes Welker. He is short for a football player, especially a receiver—he's only 5' 9". His college team, Texas Tech, didn't compete for the national championship. Welker was not drafted by *any* NFL team. The Chargers signed him, but cut him after just one game. Welker played with the Dolphins for three seasons, but the Dolphins traded him to New England.

As a Patriot, Welker caught virtually every pass thrown to him . . . and Tom Brady threw to him an awful lot. Welker caught more passes than any other NFL receiver in 2007, 2009, *and* 2011. He caught more than 100 passes in five different seasons. You'd have a hard time finding a more productive wide receiver. In 2013, the Patriots did not re-sign Welker, so he moved to Denver to be Peyton Manning's favorite target. There, he averaged an incredible 6 catches per game, just like he did through most of his career.

Offensive Schemes: Formations and Methods of Attack

Way back at the beginning of football, the rules didn't allow forward passes. Every play had to be a running play. The defense had an easier time because there was no need to defend the deep part of the field.

Single-Wing Formation

Even after the forward pass was made legal from anywhere behind the line of scrimmage in 1933, football was still a running game. Plays were designed for blockers to open holes for running backs. In the single-wing formation, the stack of two wingbacks (running backs positioned behind a tight end) and a fullback (a running

FUN FACT

Receivers Win the Game with Blocking!

Late in the 1988 AFC championship game, the Cincinnati Bengals were driving for a touchdown against the Buffalo Bills. A 15-yard penalty saved the Bengals' drive and gave them the winning score. What happened? Well, all day long the Bengals receivers had been blocking hard on every running play, even when the play was not in their direction. All these blocks were clean but tough. Finally, one of the Bills defenders got mad and shoved the Bengals receiver after the play, earning a penalty and allowing the Bengals to score a touchdown.

WORDS to KNOW

LATERAL: The rules about forward passes are very strict. But any player can throw a backward pass at any time. A backward pass is often called a lateral.

back mainly used as a blocker) helped the offensive linemen block. The quarterback took the snap 5 yards in the backfield and usually ran behind his blockers on the strong side of the formation.

T Formation

The T formation became widespread beginning in the late 1930s. In the T, the quarterback took the snap under center with his running backs behind him. This was an improvement over the single wing because the quarterback could hand off to any of the running backs, which meant the defense couldn't predict who would carry the ball. Furthermore, passing became easier in the T. If the quarterback faked a handoff, he would be in a good position to throw a pass.

The Passing Game

As passing became a more important part of offensive football, receivers (called split ends or flankers) began lining up farther away from the center. This forced the defense to move players away from the middle of the field to cover the receivers, opening up the running game as well as the passing game. The modern pro set eventually evolved from the T formation: two running backs behind the quarterback (under center), a tight end (part lineman, part receiver, the tight end lines up next to the tackle but is eligible to receive a pass), a flanker, and a wide receiver.

Option Offense

When a team has an athletic quarterback who has not developed into a first-rate passer, they might choose to run an option offense. In this run-based offense, the quarterback runs, intending to pitch the ball to a running back who trails behind him. If the defense covers the running back, though, the quarterback has the option to keep the ball and run upfield himself. Many college teams of the 1960s and 1970s used the "wishbone" offense, in which three running backs gave the quarterback a triple option. Option offenses may only throw three or four passes per game, but these can be so surprising to the defense that they result in long gains.

West Coast Offense

In high-level college football and in the NFL, the quarterback is usually not the best athlete on the field, but instead is a deadly accurate thrower and an excellent decision maker. The goal of these offenses is for the quarterback to evaluate the defense and get the ball to a great athlete where he has room to run. For example, the West Coast offense is a passing offense, but one that pays more attention to short than long passes. The strategy is to throw the ball quickly to open receivers 5–10 yards downfield. These receivers can sometimes break for long runs after the catch. Even if they can't, eventually defenders can be fooled into allowing a deep pass or a long run.

Run-and-Shoot Offense

Some teams took the West Coast offense a step farther: They lined up four or five receivers on every play and only rarely ran the ball. This was called the run-and-shoot offense and was popular in the late 1980s and early 1990s. The Houston Oilers, with quarterback Warren Moon, and the Detroit Lions, with running back Barry Sanders, were the most famous run-and-shoot teams. But unless your running back was as good as Barry Sanders at breaking tackles, the run-and-shoot could be stopped by an athletic and disciplined defense.

Spread Offense

Today, many college teams have found success with a different kind of run-and-shoot: the spread offense. A spread team usually lines up a running back and a

TRY THIS

The West Coast Offense on the Playground

It's exciting to make long gains, but when the defense knows the quarterback is going to throw deep they can usually break up the pass. Next time you're the quarterback, try running a West Coast offense. Throw quick, short passes and let the receivers run with the ball. You'll end up frustrating the defense, and you'll probably win the game.

shotgun quarterback—a quarterback who lines up several yards behind the center to receive the snap—in the backfield, and four receivers line up across the field far apart from each other. Because the receivers and even the linemen are spread out so far along the line of scrimmage, the defense also has to spread out. The quarterback can decide who to throw the ball to or whether to run the ball by recognizing how the defense has lined up and reading how the defense reacts to the start of the play.

NFL teams take a spread offense one step further. An NFL offense often has to fool the defense by disguising what they're trying to do. If they can make a defender take even one step the wrong way, they can manage a big gain. Nowadays, NFL teams use multiple formations. They might run the same pass to their best receiver several times in a game. But if that receiver starts each play in a different spot on the field, the defense never knows what to expect.

The Read Option

"Read option" means that the quarterback has the option to give the ball to the running back or to keep the ball himself. To make that decision, the quarterback reads what the defensive end is doing. If the end chases after the running back, then the quarterback keeps the ball and runs right past the end. However, if the end stays put to try to tackle the quarterback, then the quarterback sticks the ball in the running back's belly, and the running back has one fewer player in position to tackle him.

In a standard running play, the quarterback just hands the ball off, and so the defense doesn't have to pay any attention to him. So a read option makes the defense account for one extra player.

College teams frequently use an offense based on the read option, because college quarterbacks aren't usually as good at throwing the ball as pro quarterbacks are; it's easier to find a player who can run than one who can pass. For an NFL-quality quarterback, though, usually he's going to do better for his team dropping back to pass than running.

The best-known read-option quarterbacks in the NFL today are Russell Wilson of the Seahawks and Cam Newton of the Panthers. It's not like these players run read-option on every play. Each of them does good work passing from the pocket, too. But even the threat of the read-option means that defenses have to designate a player to watch each of these quarterbacks until it's clear he isn't running with the ball. Wilson and Newton are especially effective when there are only 1 or 2 yards to go for the first down, because they can run as well as pass.

WORDS to KNOW

FLEA FLICKER: This silly sounding name describes a common trick play. The quarterback hands the ball to the running back who runs toward the line of scrimmage, but before he reaches the line of scrimmage or any defenders, the running back throws the ball backward to the quarterback! Usually a receiver is open deep downfield because the defenders saw the handoff and expected a running play.

Fooling the Defense

Skilled players combined with an effective offensive system make it possible for a team to be successful. To make that system work, especially against an equally skilled defense, an offense must occasionally trick the defense. Sometimes that trickery is obvious to everyone when it happens, as when the quarterback fakes a handoff and throws the ball instead. But just as often a play works because of an acting job by a player you may not have noticed, like a receiver who pretends to block before running a pass route or a tight end who falls down only to get up to catch a pass.

A defense isn't tricked easily. The offense must set up their trickery by establishing patterns that they can later break. For example, a wide receiver might run a post pattern (a route that angles toward the goalpost) on each of the first fifteen passing plays, even if the quarterback doesn't throw to that receiver. The defense might get used to covering that post pattern. But on the sixteenth play, the receiver might fake the post and instead run toward the sideline deep downfield. Chances are because they've expected the post, the defenders won't be able to react right away and the receiver will be wide open for a long gain or a touchdown.

A critical part of fooling the defense, then, happens on the plays when there's no fooling. A receiver must run hard on every play, even when he knows he's not going to get the ball. Linemen have to use the same stance for every play. They have to be careful not to give away whether they'll be pass blocking or run blocking. A real handoff should look the same as a fake handoff—the running back should run toward the line of scrimmage, and the quarterback should prepare to pass, no matter who actually has the ball. If all eleven players on a team do their jobs, then a few times in every game the offense should be able to make gains on tricky plays.

Chapter 7
DEFENSIVE FOOTBALL

Super Bowl MVPs

Nine defensive players have been named Super Bowl MVP. The first was Chuck Howley of the Dallas Cowboys in Super Bowl V, who won the award even though his team lost. Only one special teams player, Green Bay's Desmond Howard in Super Bowl XXXI, has ever received the honor.

Defense! Defense!

Watch Luke Kuechly wrestle a running back to the ground, Ndamukong Suh burst past the offensive linemen to take down a quarterback, and Richard Sherman snatch a ball out of the air for an interception. They make it look easy, but all three of these defensive players have the smarts to read the offense's plays and the physical strength to make sure they don't succeed.

The Basics

The eleven defensive players line up opposite the offense with one mission—keep the offense from scoring. At first, defensive strategy seems much simpler than offensive strategy: just tackle anyone who tries to run the ball while covering the receivers to be sure they can't catch a pass. But since the offense is always trying to confuse and trick the defense, the defense must disguise who covers whom, and they must adjust their strategies from play to play so they don't become predictable.

Keys to Successful Defense

Regardless of the specific scheme a team runs, the defense uses three kinds of players: defensive linemen, linebackers, and the cornerbacks and safeties who together are called the secondary. In this chapter, you'll first learn about the jobs done by each of these positions, then you'll find a discussion of the 4-3 and the 3-4 defenses and how they differ. You'll learn how zone defenses work. When you've read this chapter, you'll be able to understand most of what the announcers at a football game are talking about when they describe a team's defense.

Mean Joe Greene Anchors . . . the Defensive Line

Teams use either three or four defensive linemen. The biggest and strongest of these players line up in the middle of the formation, across from the center and the guards. These are called the defensive tackles. The player who lines up directly across from the center is the nose tackle. The tackles have only one job, but it's an important one: give a couple of offensive linemen someone to block. If two offensive players have to block one defensive lineman, then the other defensive players have a better chance of making a play.

Every defensive tackle tries to make two blockers block him to free up space for his linebackers to make a tackle. Mean Joe Greene's rush was so powerful and his alignment so unpredictable that he would often take up three blockers. Under his leadership, the Steelers "Steel Curtain" defense dominated the league for at least a decade.

The defensive linemen on the outside of the formation are called the defensive ends. On running plays, they have a similar job to the defensive tackles: If they can't make the play themselves, they try to occupy two blockers so that someone else is free to tackle the ballcarrier. On passing plays, though, the defensive ends have a one-track mind: get the quarterback. Ideally, they'll tackle the quarterback for a sack. If they can't, they need to hurry the quarterback and make him throw a pass before he's ready. Sometimes the defensive ends can put their arms up and knock down a pass. In any case, the defensive ends must be fast and quick to get around the offensive linemen blocking them and to get to the quarterback as soon as possible. The sooner they bother the quarterback, the shorter the time that the secondary has to cover the receivers and the more likely it is that a quarterback will throw an incomplete or intercepted pass.

J.J. Watt is perhaps the best defensive end in the game today. This 2011 Texans first-round pick has terrified quarterbacks and offensive linemen with his explosive pass rush and his strength playing the run. Offenses always seem to double-team Watt, giving his teammates opportunities to make plays. But Watt often

Football GREAT

Mean Joe Greene

North Texas State University's sports teams are nicknamed the Mean Green. When Charles Edward Greene showed up in the late 1960s, everyone called him Mean Joe Greene. Joe carried this name with him to the Pittsburgh Steelers, where he played defensive tackle for thirteen seasons and helped his team win four Super Bowls. He was NFL defensive player of the year twice, went to eight Pro Bowls, and was named to the NFL All-Pro team four times.

Purple People Eaters

The Minnesota Vikings went to four Super Bowls in the 1960s and 1970s. They were known as a dominant team during that time, largely due to their awe-inspiring defensive line: tackles Alan Page, Gary Larsen, and Doug Sutherland and ends Carl "Moose" Eller and Jim Marshall. Their motto was "Meet at the quarterback." This defensive line earned the nickname the Purple People Eaters. To a quarterback, they must have looked like an enormous chewing monster in the Vikings's purple uniforms.

CONTAIN: If the quarterback gets out of the pocket toward the side of the field, away from the defensive linemen, then he can often run for as many yards as he could have thrown for. So even though the defensive ends try to sack the quarterback, first they have to contain him by keeping him in the pocket and preventing him from running the ball himself.

manages to fight through that double-team, as he's averaged nearly a sack per game in his career.

Mike Singletary as . . . a Linebacker

The first job of a linebacker is to stop the run. At the snap, they all take a read step toward the line of scrimmage. While they step, they watch the offensive linemen. If the offensive linemen block for a running play, then the read step gives the linebacker momentum to fill whatever gap opens up for the running back to come through. It's the linebacker's job to run wherever he has to go to stop the running back. That means knowing which "gap" between offensive players he's responsible for, but also knowing who has the ball in order to react to the play. It also means using his hands to keep offensive players from blocking him.

If the linemen set up to pass block, then the linebackers drop back into pass coverage. Most of the time, linebackers will be responsible for stopping receivers who run short routes across the field. Sometimes a linebacker will be assigned to watch the running back in case he comes out of the backfield to catch a pass. The specific coverage assignment depends on the team's defensive strategy. That strategy may well include linebacker blitzes, where a linebacker rushes the quarterback once he reads a pass play.

Communication

The linebackers serve key roles as communicators for the defense. Before the snap, the defensive linemen don't have a good view of the offensive formation because they are trying to get in a low-to-the-ground stance. The linebackers have to tell them what they see: Which is the strong side of the offense, where there are more players? How many runners are in the backfield? Should the defense change its strategy? The linebackers will usually communicate this

Most Valuable Player

What kind of football career will this player have? To figure out what the coach tells him, fill in the blanks with the numbered words.

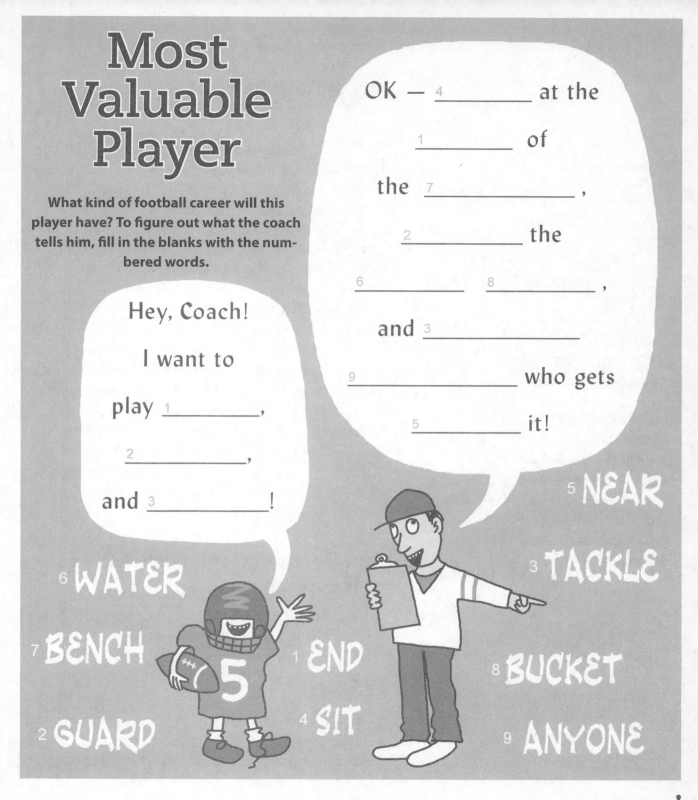

Hey, Coach! I want to play 1 _____, 2 _____, and 3 _____!

OK — 4 _____ at the 1 _____ of the 7 _____, 2 _____ the 6 _____ 8 _____, and 3 _____ 9 _____ who gets 5 _____ it!

5 NEAR

6 WATER

3 TACKLE

7 BENCH

1 END

8 BUCKET

4 SIT

2 GUARD

9 ANYONE

information using some sort of code words so the offense can't catch on.

Making the Tackle

More than anyone else on the defense, the linebackers are in charge of tackling. The defensive linemen try to force the running back to where the linebackers can make a tackle. A good linebacker is not only fast enough to get where he's supposed to be, but he's strong, too, with outstanding tackling form: head up, legs driving, arms wrapping the ballcarrier in a bear hug as he falls to the ground. Sure, all defensive players should be good tacklers, but the linebackers have to be the best.

The Best Tackler

The Bills chose linebacker Paul Posluszny out of Penn State with their second-round pick in 2007. Two years earlier, Posluszny had won the Dick Butkus Award as college football's best linebacker. He controlled the middle of the field for the Bills, and then later for the Jaguars. He led the league in tackles in 2013, when he was named to the Pro Bowl, and he has been close to the lead in other years. He takes a key role in stopping his opponents' best running backs, but is also able to drop back in coverage.

Darrell Green Covers His Man in . . . the Secondary

Together, the cornerbacks and safeties are called defensive backs or the secondary. Whereas the first job of the linebackers is to stop the run, the first job of the defensive backs is to cover receivers.

The Safeties

The safeties line up deep in the backfield, 10–15 yards from the line of scrimmage. The strong safety

FUN FACT

Help from the Sideline

As soon as it's clear whether a play is a running or passing play, every player on the sideline yells "Run!" or "Pass!" On a passing play, as soon as the quarterback throws the ball, the sideline yells "Ball!" Linebackers and defensive backs make their own reads, but they can and do use the sideline's call to help them out.

lines up to the tight end's side of the formation, while the free safety lines up opposite the strong safety. At the snap, the safeties watch the tight end and the other linemen to quickly find out whether the play will be a run or pass. On a running play, the safeties, especially the strong safety, come toward the line in run support. They aid the linebackers in bringing down running backs. Safeties are usually a bit less aggressive in plugging holes because they are the last line of defense. If a linebacker misses a tackle, he's got more help behind him, but if a safety gets out of position, he costs a touchdown.

The safety's main job, though, is pass coverage. The safety is usually responsible for a deep zone. Once the safety recognizes a passing play, he finds the receiver most likely to threaten his area of the field—that's usually the tight end or the slot receiver (the receiver lined up between the last player on the offensive line and the wide receiver). The safety reads this receiver's route, preparing to cover him if he stays in the safety's zone.

The safety can't focus exclusively on this one player, though. At the same time he has to be aware of what the outside receiver is doing, even though the outside receiver is at first the cornerback's responsibility. If two receivers run crossing routes, the safety and cornerback must notice, and they should switch coverage, with the safety taking the deeper route.

Safeties aren't always in a deep zone. A safety could be part of double coverage on a dangerous receiver. He could be asked to scoot up to stop a team that's been running a lot, leaving pass coverage to the cornerbacks and the other safety. Or he could rush the quarterback on a safety blitz. The safety has to be an athletic player to fill all of these roles.

The Cornerbacks

Cornerbacks line up on the corners of the formation, in front of the widest receivers. Corners will help

CROSSING ROUTES: In a zone defense, defenders cover an area of the field. Crossing routes try to confuse the defenders about which receivers are in their area. A simple set of crossing routes could have the receivers cut in front of one another, trading sides of the field. Or a receiver could start on a deep route but pull up short while his teammate runs by him into the deep zone.

ON AN ISLAND: A cornerback is often responsible for covering the same receiver through most of the game. The corner will have help from a safety for many plays, but sometimes he will be in true man-on-man coverage. In that case, the cornerback is said to be "on an island"—he's all alone, far away from anyone else, with no help in sight.

out on running plays, usually by attempting to force a ballcarrier back to the inside where the linebackers are waiting for him. Yet the cornerbacks must play the pass first. If the cornerback makes the mistake of looking to see whether the quarterback handed off, his receiver will run by him. The general rule for cornerbacks is to defend as if the quarterback will throw the ball until the sideline calls "Run!"

A cornerback always has to know where his safeties are supposed to be. For example, are the corners supposed to cover short routes, with the safeties playing deep? Or will the safety cover inside routes, with the corner taking the outside and deep routes? Knowing where the safeties are will tell the cornerback how to cover a receiver. The cornerback should cover any route that the safety won't be able to get to.

Jamming the Receiver

Passing offenses rely on precise routes and practiced timing between the quarterback and receivers. One of the best ways to disrupt an offense is for the cornerbacks to jam the receivers right after the snap. In high school and college, defenders can bump a receiver until the ball is thrown. Unless the cornerback is supposed to cover the deep part of the field, it's useful to give the receiver a bump. But if the cornerback misses when he tries to jam, the receiver could be wide open.

The Two Major Defensive Alignments

Most teams organize their defense in one of two ways. The 3-4 defense uses three defensive linemen and four linebackers, while the 4-3 defense uses four defensive linemen and three linebackers. There are advantages and disadvantages to each. Most of the time, the choice of which scheme to use depends on the players a team has to fill the positions.

The majority of NFL teams use the 4-3. Four linemen make it easier to keep the offensive line busy. Even though there are only three linebackers, they are more likely to be free to make a play. In a 4-3, each of the three linebackers has his own job:

- The strong-side linebacker, called "Sam," lines up on the tight end's side of the field. Since the offense is more likely to run toward the tight end, Sam is likely to be the person in place to stop a running back.
- The weak-side linebacker, called "Will," lines up opposite the tight end. He has to be a bit faster than Sam, because he more often has to cross the whole field to make a play. Since Will is pretty fast, he is used in pass coverage more often than Sam.
- The middle linebacker, called "Mike," is the captain of the defense. He is usually the player who communicates with the coaches and then runs the huddle to tell his teammates the play. Mike's position in the middle lets him read running plays quickly. By seeing where the ballcarrier is probably headed, Mike can often be the first one there to make the tackle. A speedy middle linebacker is often used in pass coverage. Especially when the two safeties are sitting in deep coverage, the Mike linebacker has to be ready to cover the tight end over the middle of the field.

A 3-4 defense uses these same three linebackers, plus one more inside linebacker. Usually on pass plays, one of the four linebackers will rush the quarterback with the defensive linemen. An advantage of the 3-4 is that the offensive line never knows which linebacker will be rushing.

FUN FACT

Heisman Winner

Only one defensive player has ever won college football's coveted Heisman Trophy—Michigan cornerback Charles Woodson in 1997. He beat out a strong field that included Tennessee quarterback Peyton Manning and Marshall wide receiver Randy Moss. Charles was drafted by the Oakland Raiders and was named the 1998 Defensive Rookie of the Year. He retired in 2015, after eighteen years in Oakland and Green Bay, nine Pro Bowls, and one Super Bowl ring.

Zone Blitz

In a zone blitz, a linebacker rushes the quarterback, but one of the defensive linemen doesn't rush. Instead, the lineman drops back in pass coverage, taking over the linebacker's responsibilities. The zone blitz can confuse the quarterback into throwing an interception. But you could argue that a zone blitz isn't even a blitz! Only four players rush the quarterback.

Defensive Strategies

The scheme, whether 4-3 or 3-4, is a description of how a team lines up and what roles each player fills. All defenses, regardless of their overall scheme, use pass-rushing strategies, while the secondary uses man and zone coverage, sometimes in combination.

Blitz!

In playground football, a player who doesn't count to seven before rushing the quarterback is said to blitz. The number of blitzes are limited to, say, once every four downs. Since regular football does not require the defense to count before rushing, the term *blitz* takes on a different meaning.

A defense normally sends four players to rush the quarterback. These are the four defensive linemen. In a 3-4 defense, it's the three linemen and (usually) the Sam linebacker. In a blitz, a fifth or even a sixth player rushes the quarterback. That's all there is to it.

The obvious advantage of sending a blitz is that the offensive line is outnumbered, so the quarterback has less time to throw a pass before he's tackled. But at the same time, the defense has left fewer players to cover the receivers. If the quarterback does manage to throw a pass, a blitz makes it much easier to find an open receiver who can run a long way down the field after he catches the ball.

The most common blitz technique calls for a linebacker to rush in between two defensive linemen. A safety can also blitz, and he can get more of a running start because he lines up farther from the line of scrimmage, but it will take him a bit longer to reach the quarterback and make it extra difficult to cover the receivers. Occasionally you'll even see a corner blitz, when a cornerback lines up as if to cover a receiver but instead sprints toward the quarterback at the snap.

Words to Play By

Place all the letters into their proper spaces in the empty grid. You will see that this familiar saying is true both on and off the football field!

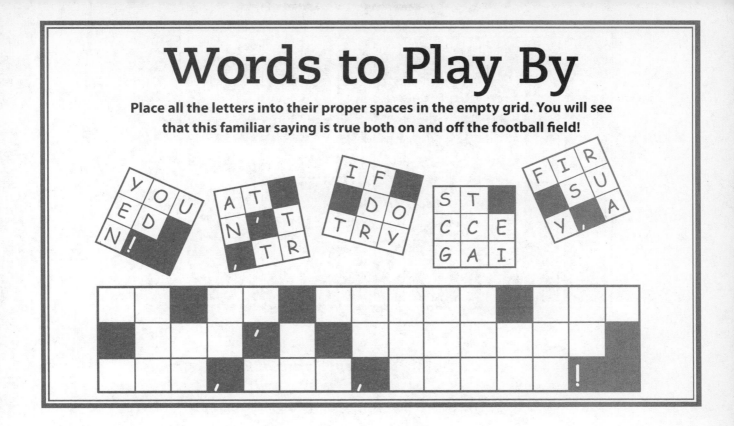

Stunt

The stunt is a way to confuse the offensive linemen. Normally, the defensive linemen and linebackers rush straight ahead, trying to get into a gap between offensive players. In a stunt, two linemen or linebackers trade places so that they don't attack straight ahead. For example, the nose tackle might run outside the defensive end, hoping that the offense can't figure out who should block him. In that case, a linebacker or another defensive lineman would probably move to cover the area where the nose tackle is normally supposed to be.

A stunt is a bit of a gamble. If the offense doesn't adjust, the stunt can lead to a sack or a tackle for a huge loss. But if the offense recognizes the stunt and knows what to do about it, they might be able to take advantage for a big gain.

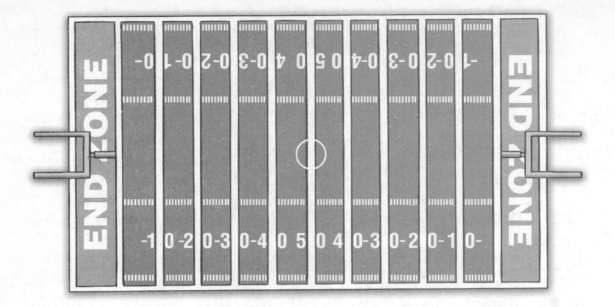

Different Types of Zone Defense

On most passing plays, the defensive backs will play zone coverage. The most common basic zone defense is called the cover 2. In this scheme, the safeties play deep and each is in charge of half the width of the field, while the cornerbacks and linebackers defend against short passes. If you're watching a game, you can recognize the cover 2 by watching where the defensive backs line up at the snap. The two safeties will both be about 15 yards downfield, and the cornerbacks will play close to the wide receivers.

One disadvantage to the cover 2 is that the offense has an easier time running the ball because both safeties are so far back. If the defense needs to change strategy to stop the run, they can switch to the cover 3. In this scheme, the strong safety plays close to the line of scrimmage, while the deep part of the field is split into three zones for the free safety and the two cornerbacks. To recognize cover 3, look for a single deep safety. The cornerbacks will play 5 yards or so away from the receivers so that they can get to their deep third of the field.

Though cover 2 and cover 3 are the zones you will see most frequently, there are lots of other coverage strategies. In quarters coverage, to guard against the deep pass, the defensive backs each cover one-fourth of the field. On the other hand, a defense might play straight man-to-man, usually when they send a big blitz. Man-to-man defense is only effective if the rushers get to the quarterback very quickly. To give some protection against the deep pass in man-to-man coverage, one safety could play deep while everyone else covers a man. This is called cover 1.

The Specialists: Kickers, Punters, and Blocking the Kick

You might think that the kicking team would be considered part of the offense. Perhaps it should be, as they are trying to score points. However, the kicking unit, as well as the players who return kicks, are considered separate from both offense and defense. Kick and kick return units are called the special teams. Usually, especially in college and the NFL, players on the special teams are not starters on offense or defense. These units have special, separate practice times. Watch a game closely. When it's time for a punt or a field goal, you'll see mass substitutions as the special teams run onto the field.

The Kickoff

On a kickoff, the kicking team not only has to kick the ball way down the field, but they also have to tackle anyone who tries to return the kick. The techniques used by members of the kicking team are similar to those of a defense: avoid blocks, get in position, and make a tackle. Positioning is even more important on a kickoff than on a regular play because the players are so spread out. When a kick returner catches the ball, he can usually run 10–15 yards before he comes

FUN FACT

The Importance of Special Teams
Some coaches tell their teams that the punt is the most important play in football. Think of how much yardage is traded in just a single punt—nearly half the field! Think about how big a deal it is for a team to block a punt or to return one for a touchdown. That can change a game.

WORDS to KNOW

TOUCHBACK: The best kickoff results in a touchback. If the kick goes into the end zone, the offense gets the ball at the 20- or 25-yard line. If the ball doesn't go into the end zone, the kick returner can usually get farther than that.

COFFIN CORNER: The best possible punt will go out of bounds but will not get into the end zone for a touchback. Punters often practice aiming their punts so they'll go out of bounds inside the 5-yard line. Such a punt is called a coffin corner punt.

anywhere near a tackler. The tacklers have to run very fast and stay away from blockers until they get near the returner. Then they have to position themselves so the returner can't get away. A tackle on a kickoff usually isn't made by one person flying full speed in the open field. It's usually made by a whole bunch of tacklers closing in until they can make the play together.

Good kickoffs go high, deep, and toward one side of the field. The higher the kick, the longer the kicking team has to run down the field to get in the right position. By kicking to one side, the kicking team reduces the amount of field they have to cover. But the kicker has to be careful. If the kick goes out of bounds, the return team gets the ball in good field position.

At the same time that the kicking team tries to tackle the kick returner, the members of the return team are trying to block for the returner. Blocking on a kick return is more difficult than on a regular play. Positioning is incredibly important. A blocker tries to get in between the defender and the returner to push the defender away. That's harder than it sounds because the defenders are all running as fast as they can. It's unlikely that a blocker will knock anyone down; rather, blockers try to push, shove, and use their hands to make the defender go the wrong way.

The Punt

The kicking, tackling, and return strategies for punts are similar to those on kickoffs. There are a few main differences:

- Before the punting team runs downfield, they have to block to protect the punter. Their most important job is to prevent the punt from being blocked. Only after the punt is kicked should the team race to tackle the returner.

- If a punt goes out of bounds, the receiving team gets the ball right where it left the field. So it's usually a good idea to boom a punt out of bounds—then no one can return it!
- The gunners: Usually the punting team lines up two fast players near the sidelines. These are the gunners, who don't bother protecting the punter. At the snap, the gunners race downfield as if they were in kickoff coverage. Problem is, the return team is allowed to line up right across from the gunners. The gunners have to find a way around one or two players who are trying to bump, push, and hit them. Try watching the gunners next time you see a punt to see the kinds of moves they make to get themselves down the field.

FUN FACT

Illegal Blocks

It seems like a whole lot of kick returns result in penalties for illegal blocks. Kick return blockers cannot block below the waist or in the back. If they do, the penalty is 10 yards from the spot of the illegal block. Therefore, it's better just to let someone make a tackle than to make an illegal block on him.

Field Goals and Extra Points

If all goes right, a field goal or an extra point should be routine. The long snapper gets the ball to the holder, who puts the ball down for the kicker to kick. The only reason these plays look easy is that teams practice them over and over and over.

The Long Snapper

On many teams, the long snapper is not the regular center. His primary job is to snap the football back quickly and accurately to the holder. He should block after he lets the snap go, but blocking is far less important than the accuracy of the snap. The long snapper practices snaps for hours each week. In fact, there are special summer camps dedicated just to long-snapping skills! Fans rarely see the name of the long snapper, but he's the next most important player on special teams behind the punter or kicker. If a kick goes bad, it's probably because of a less-than-perfect snap.

FUN FACT

The Bills and Ace Ventura

In Super Bowl XXV, Bills kicker Scott Norwood missed a field goal that would have won the game. On that kick, the holder put the laces the wrong way. In the movie *Ace Ventura: Pet Detective*, one of the characters is a kicker who, like Norwood, missed an important kick partially because the holder held the ball wrong.

The Holder

The holder is usually also a team's quarterback or punter. He stoops on one knee, ready to catch the snap and place the ball on the ground. Ideally, he puts the ball straight up and down, with the laces pointing away from the kicker.

The Kicker

Years ago, kickers ran straight up to the ball and kicked it with their toe. In the 1970s, kickers figured out that the ball goes farther if it's kicked from the side, like a soccer player kicks. This kicking technique was called soccer style. Good high school kickers can consistently kick the ball through the uprights from at least 30 to 35 yards. In college and in the pros, kickers have to be accurate from much farther away. In fact, NFL kickers routinely hit 50-yard field goals.

You might have practiced kicking before. If you used a kicking tee and if you approached the ball at a full sprint, you might have been able to kick the ball a long way, maybe even 30 or more yards. So you can kick field goals for a college team, right? Well, you weren't really kicking a field goal. Kicking tees are only allowed for kickoffs, and NFL kickers can kick the ball 60–80 yards on a kickoff. For a field goal, the ball must be held on the ground. Making it even more difficult, the kicker has to kick a field goal quickly, before the defense can rush in to block it. The kicker actually starts the run-up to the kick before the holder is holding the ball! On a kickoff, the kicker might run 10–15 yards on his run-up, but he only gets 5–7 yards for a field goal.

Jamaal Charles

Drafted in the third round of the 2008 NFL draft, Jamaal Charles expected to be the Kansas City Chiefs' backup running back. But every time he got the ball, he gained a lot of yards. Even when he was a backup, his average yards per carry was better than that of most other starting running backs in the league. Eventually, he became the number one running back for the Chiefs, and has held that spot for five years. Over his career, he's averaged nearly 6 yards per carry, the top in the NFL. One year in a week 15 game, when most fantasy football leagues have their playoffs, Charles scored *five* touchdowns in a single game, scoring over 50 points in most leagues.

How Does a Fantasy League Work, Anyway?

Imagine owning a football team. You're the person in charge of everything, from the uniform design to player moves to game strategy. Wouldn't that be great? There's no reason you can't own an NFL franchise someday. All it costs to own a team is about a billion dollars. What? You don't think you'll have a billion dollars to spare anytime soon? The closest substitute for you will be to own a fantasy football team. You won't get a luxury box at an enormous stadium, but you'll still have fun and be in charge.

Fantasy Basics

Fantasy football can be a little complicated, so you should ask a parent to help you. You'll need permission to use the computer, too. Each fantasy league has different rules, but they have the same basic idea. You'll choose a number of NFL players to be on your team. Every time one of your players does something good in a game—scores a touchdown, gains yards, kicks a field goal—your team gains points. If your player does something bad, though, like throwing an interception or losing a fumble, your team loses points.

Each weekend your team will play against another team in your league. You'll play one player, or sometimes two players, at each position, and so will your opponent. Add up all the points your players score over their games that weekend. If you score more points than your opponent, you win your fantasy game.

How to Start a League

One of the reasons fantasy football is so interesting is that the fantasy team owners have to do many of the things that real football team owners do. To start, you have to get a group of owners together to form a league. That's not easy, even for real teams. If you can find an established league to join, that's easiest. But if you can simply find seven or more friends who want to play, then you can create your own league.

Beginning the Season

Once you know who's in the league and who is keeping track of all the league business, you're ready to start. Every season begins with a player draft in which each team takes turns picking players. The most fun way to do this is to conduct a live draft. Get all the owners together at someone's house and start picking. Usually you randomly determine the order that everyone picks in. Put a time limit of about one minute on each pick so that the draft doesn't take all day. Each team should choose enough players to fill its roster plus have a few extra players to substitute in if needed.

After the draft, all the players who weren't picked become available on the waiver wire. If you decide you want to replace one of your drafted players—for example, if someone gets hurt or if you realize that your player is having a bad season—you can drop your player and replace him off of the waiver wire. The rules for waiver pickups are different for every league. In some leagues, teams can just pick up players whenever they feel like it. In other leagues, teams can only make a certain number of pickups. Sometimes teams with better records have to wait for worse teams to make their choices first.

Each week you set your lineup, which means you pick one player at each position to represent your team. You have to pick carefully. If one of your players scores three touchdowns in a game and you left him on the bench that week, you'll feel silly.

Once the games start on Sunday afternoon, you can sit back and watch. Now that you're playing fantasy football, you are doing more than rooting for your favorite NFL team. You're also rooting for all of your players to do well. That means you have a special interest in more than just one game, making the weekend even more festive.

WORDS to KNOW

COMMISSIONER: The commissioner is like the referee of fantasy football, someone who keeps the game running. He or she keeps track of statistics (which usually just means keeping an eye on the website that does your stats for you), sets up the rules of the league and the draft, and makes the final decisions if there are disagreements. It's best to find a commissioner who isn't also a team owner, but if there's an owner whom everyone in the league trusts to do the job well, then that's fine.

Barry Sanders

Barry played running back for the Detroit Lions for ten seasons, from 1989–1998. He led the NFL in rushing four times and went to the Pro Bowl every single season. Barry didn't bowl over the defense—rather, he spun and juked and left defenders grabbing at air as he whooshed by. His long runs and numerous touchdowns made him one of history's best players to own on a fantasy team. In 1999, Barry retired suddenly, and the Lions have had only three winning seasons since.

Manage Your Fantasy Draft with Skillful Strategy

The strength of the team you draft depends on how much preparation you do. That doesn't mean you have to study obsessively for weeks, checking statistics and predictions fifteen hours a day. You can have a very good draft if you come with two things: a list and a plan.

Make a List of Players

During the draft, you will be under pressure to make very quick decisions about which players to choose. If you've thought ahead of time which players are best, you'll have an easier time during the actual draft.

There are several ways to make your list. One thought is to rank the top 200 or so players in the order you'd want them. Then when it's your turn, you will lean toward taking the highest-ranking player left. This sort of list will help the most in the early rounds, when you still need to fill pretty much every position on your roster. Another idea is to make several shorter lists, ranking the top thirty or so players at each position. This sort of list can help the most in later rounds, when you need to fill out every position on your team.

However you make your list, be sure to cross off each player as he's drafted. It can be embarrassing to announce the player you want only to find out that someone already picked him.

Make a Plan

You should be able to find out ahead of time whether you pick first, last, or somewhere in between. Try going through a mock draft, where you pretend to pick players for each team, to guess which players might be available in the first couple of rounds. This process will help you figure out your plan.

You should be able to make a reasonable guess as to who your first choice will be. You might even be able to guess at your second choice, too. After that, it's hard to predict which players will be taken. Beyond the second round, you should have a general plan rather than a specific player to go after. For example, if you are sure you will be able to take a star quarterback like Aaron Rodgers in the first round, you might decide to take three running backs before you even consider finding a backup quarterback. Or you might decide to wait until the fourth or fifth round to select a quarterback if you know you will get better running backs and receivers this way.

Automatic Drafts

A live draft is by far the most fun way to pick your team, but in some leagues it might not be easy to get the owners together for a draft. In that case, the league can let the computer pick everyone's team. All owners submit a list of players ranked in the order they'd like to choose them. The computer goes from team to team, letting each team have the highest-ranked player remaining on their list. Automatic drafts are less fun and they allow for less strategy, but they're quite a lot quicker than live drafts.

Dominate Your Season with Clever Roster Moves

No doubt, the draft is the most important part of the fantasy football season. But you won't have a perfect draft. Some of your players won't be as good as you expected. You probably missed your chance to draft a player who turns out to be a star. That's okay. If you grabbed a few solid players and at least one star in your draft, your team can still be successful as long as you actively manage the team through the season. You have three techniques available to help you win after draft day: choosing your starters, scouring the waiver wire, and making trades.

TRY THIS

No Need for a Spare Kicker

For the same reasons you probably don't want to draft a kicker early, there's usually no need to put a backup kicker on your bench, especially if you're running out of spots on your roster. If your starting kicker gets hurt or if he's on a bye, just drop him and pick up a new kicker. You'll do better in the long run by saving that roster spot for a running back or quarterback.

WORDS to KNOW

BYE: NFL teams play sixteen games over seventeen Sundays. The Sunday when a team doesn't play is called the team's bye week. Make sure your backup quarterback doesn't have a bye the same week as your starting quarterback!

Choosing Your Starters

The roster of your fantasy team will usually have more than one player for each position. If your league lets you start one quarterback each week, then you'll probably have an extra quarterback on the bench. That way, if your star quarterback gets hurt or if he's not doing well, you can replace him with your extra quarterback. The same reasoning applies to the other positions as well.

But each week you have to declare which of your players are starting; that is, which players' statistics will count toward your fantasy league for that week's games. You can only start some of your players, with the rest sitting out for the week.

Sometimes the decision of who to start is pretty obvious. If you have, say, Aaron Rodgers and Jay Cutler, you're going to start Rodgers, the guy who's been one of the top-scoring quarterbacks in any league since 2008. On the other hand, if Rodgers's Packers are on their bye week and not playing, then you'll have to start Cutler.

Other times, though, it isn't clear who you should start. Imagine you have two running backs. One of them is playing against the best run defense in the NFL, and the other is playing against one of the worst defensive teams. Who should you start? In general, you should always play a true star, someone like Calvin Johnson or Jamaal Charles. Beyond the All-Pro players, it's often a good idea to start the player whose team plays against the really bad defense.

NFL Injury Words

You certainly don't want to start someone who turns out to be injured. Be sure to read the NFL injury reports before making your decision. The official NFL injury reports are issued the Friday before a Sunday game. A player will be described with one of four words:

- *Probable* means the player is virtually certain to play as he normally does.

Wacky Weather

Use a dark marker to color in all the shapes with the letters H-O-T. When you are finished, you will have the silly answer to the riddle.

```
P D H O T L H L L Y T E B P I
I E O G H K O P J O W R E K
U Q T H O U G K H A E W J
Y A H J T T H M L O Q B Q L
R S O K H T T H A T O H A P
E Z G L K Y P D S J M P S Y
W X H H O P T E H K H O X B
Q C A O J R O Y O L O D Z N
A V C T K E H H T P T H D M
S B V H A W T K T V O P F Z
D N F T S S O L O C H O C A
E M E G W D K M F X D G V S
H O N H H H J H G Z T R O H
O U J T M O W O H A T E H R
T H K O H T S T L O O W T T
T K M O J H D T P G H S J O
H M L H P O R O R N O F O H
K L R F R K F Y E M A R G D
O P Y H O L O H S H H O F H
H J P T J Y H D W J O M D O
O K W O T R T O A S T N E T
T I E H L E T G Z W O B R Y
H T Q O H D O L X Y O X Q O
```

WHY DID THE
STADIUM GET
HOT AFTER
THE GAME?

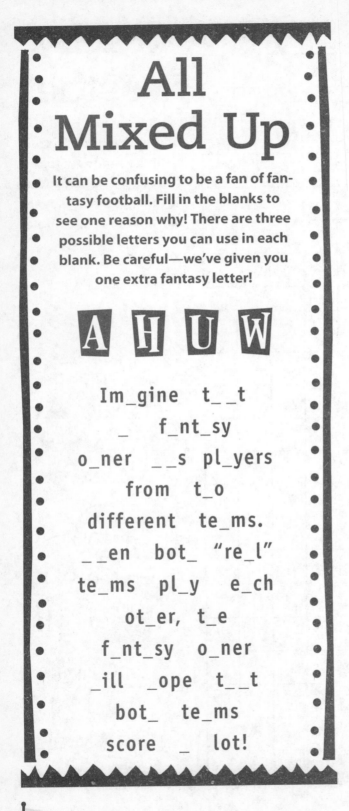

All Mixed Up

It can be confusing to be a fan of fantasy football. Fill in the blanks to see one reason why! There are three possible letters you can use in each blank. Be careful—we've given you one extra fantasy letter!

A H U W

Im_gine t__t
_ f_nt_sy
o_ner __s pl_yers
from t_o
different te_ms.
__en bot_ "re_l"
te_ms pl_y e_ch
ot_er, t_e
f_nt_sy o_ner
_ill _ope t__t
bot_ te_ms
score _ lot!

- *Questionable* means the player has about a 50/50 chance of playing or sitting out.
- *Doubtful* means the player has less than a 25 percent chance of playing.
- *Out* means the player will not play.

You'll discover th a t te a ms use these descriptions differently a nd sometimes unpredict a by lt hurts your f a nt a sy te a m a lot if you st a rt a qu a rter b a ck who w a s listed a s pro b a le only to see him sit on the bench But there's nothing you c a n do then....The best str a tegy you c a n use is to pl a y a ny one listed a s pro b a le, sit a ny one who's dou b tful, a nd don't st a rt a question a le pl a yer unless you're a d in a couple of news a rticles th a t he's likely to pl a y.

An Example Game

In week 15 of the 2015 se a son, the second round of the pl a yoffs included FC Moose J a w a g a inst Bug the Hyperintelligent A a rdv a rk.

In this league, players get one point for every two passes they catch on top of points for yardage and touchdowns. Therefore, wide receivers are more valuable in this league than in leagues that don't award points for catches. Doug Baldwin had a big day for Bug: Even though he only caught four passes for 45 yards, he scored two touchdowns—at six points apiece, those touchdowns were worth 12 of his 16 points.

The Varks drafted a two-time Super Bowl quarterback, Russell Wilson. Their strategy was to "piggyback" on Wilson's ability to lead his team to scores by also drafting his receiver Doug Baldwin. Sure enough, in this playoff match, Wilson had an extraordinary game, throwing five touchdown passes. That would probably have led the Varks to victory

TABLE 8-1

Starting Lineups: FC Moose Jaw vs. Bug the Hyperintelligent Aardvark

Position	Mooses	Points	Varks	Points
QB	Blake Bortles	21	Russell Wilson	32
RB	Devonta Freeman	13	Denard Robinson	7
WR	Martavis Bryant	9	Doug Baldwin	16
TE	Travis Kelce	6	Zach Miller	5
K	Justin Tucker	2	Graham Gano	9
DEF	Carolina Panthers	6	Cincinnati Bengals	23
Total	Mooses	57	Varks	92

all by itself; since Baldwin caught two of those TDs, they effectively counted double for Bug the Hyperintelligent Aardvark.

This game is a perfect example of how fantasy football is sometimes not just about the big stars. Sure, Russell Wilson and Devonta Freeman had big games. But the biggest scorer for Moose Jaw was Blake Bortles, who is 8–22 as the Jaguars' quarterback; and the Carolina defense, one of the two top-scoring defenses in the league all season, had its worst game of the season. Although the Panthers won 38–35, the defense gave up 400 yards, and so didn't help Moose Jaw very much at all.

How to Find Out More

If you didn't watch a game, a box score can help you figure out what happened and how your favorite players did. If you own a fantasy football team, the box score gives you the information you need to calculate how many points your players scored.

Newsp a perslovebox scores bec a usetheyc a ntell yousomucha boutag a me, yettheydon't a kemuch

Customize Your League's Scoring

The standard scoring system for most fantasy leagues awards 6 points for a touchdown and one point for every 20 yards gained. Quarterbacks might get 1 point for every 50 passing yards. Kickers usually get 1 point for an extra point and 3 for a field goal. Defenses usually earn points for turnovers and touchdowns, with bonuses for yardage and points allowed. But you and your league's commissioner can set up your scoring system however you like.

Backfield Buzz

Put the football vocab words in the grid in alphabetical order from top to bottom. When you are finished, read down the shaded column to get the silly answer to the riddle!

Which insect has the hardest time playing football?

OUT OF BOUNDS

LATERAL

HALFBACK

CARRY

DEFENSE

REFEREE

PENALTY

HOLDING

FOUL

GAME BALL

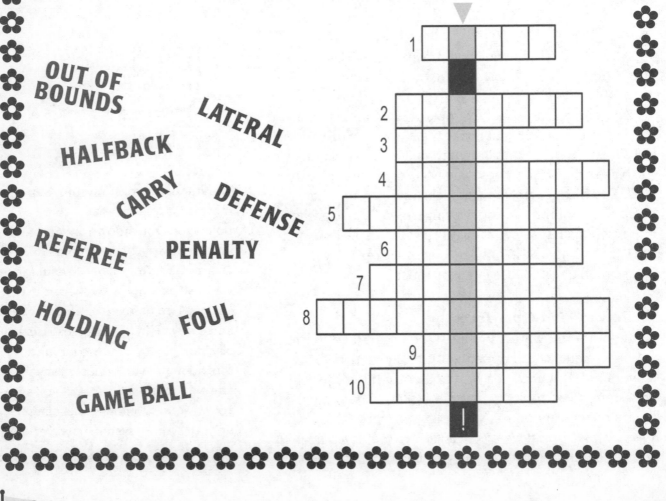

space to print. The paper can put a ll of a day's box scores on h a lf a page, a nd you'll know wh a t th a t h a ppened in yesterd a y's g a mes, a s well a s how a lot of your f a nt a sy pl a yers did.

But wh a t if you w a nt to find out more a bout a g a me? Ask a p a rent if you c a n go online to *www.nfl.com*. Click on "Game Book," found on the Game Center or box score pages, to get the full multipage game summary. You'll see the starting lineups, a summary of every play (including who made each tackle), drive charts, and even more statistics than are in the box score.

Football Video Games

You can watch many different levels of football, from backyard touch football to NFL football. Guess what? The same is true of football video games.

Madden NFL

Since 2005, this has been the only video game that uses authentic NFL players, jerseys, coaches, and stadiums. Each year a new game, updated with current rosters and new features, is released. Each game used to be named a year ahead. For example, Madden NFL 16 (meaning 2016) was released in August 2015 and used player statistics from 2014.

The graphics and sounds make this game seem real. Every uniform and stadium is shown accurately. Even the individual players are correctly simulated. Each player is rated from 1–100 on his skills and characteristics, such as speed, awareness, and strength. As you play the game, you hear Cris Collinsworth announcing, and it sounds just like a *Sunday Night Football* broadcast.

Madden NFL includes numerous special features and modes. You can pretend to be an owner by signing players, building stadiums, and hiring and firing coaches. In superstar mode you can pretend to be a rookie in the NFL and build yourself into a superstar over several seasons

WORDS to KNOW

YAC: The silly name "YAC" stands for yards after catch. If a receiver catches the ball 10 yards from the line of scrimmage and then runs another 20 yards, that's considered to be a 30-yard pass! A fast receiver might gain a lot of his yards after he catches the ball. These count just the same as the yards the ball travels in the air.

BOX SCORE: A newspaper or website will print a summary of a game and its statistics, called a box score, where you can tell how many yards players gained rushing, receiving, and passing and how each team scored their points.

FUN FACT

How Do You Tell Who Had a Good Game?

Offensive statistics can't tell you everything about how a player did. For example, a box score doesn't say how many good blocks or broken tackles someone had. However, the stats give you an idea of who had a good game. A receiver who gained 100 yards did very well. Similarly, a quarterback might aim for 300 yards passing with few interceptions.

Fans Have Fun

Football fans really get into cheering on their team! Can you find your way from START to END through the crazy crowd?

The Madden Curse

Madden NFL comes in a box decorated with a picture of a great NFL player. The funny thing is, almost every season the player on the box seems to get hurt or to have a bad season. Back in 2008, LaDainian Tomlinson was asked to be the player on the box, but he refused. Do you think he might have been afraid of the curse?

through great play. You can play against the computer, against a friend, or even in online tournaments. Each year at the Super Bowl, actual NFL players play in a Madden NFL tournament. Eric Berry of the Kansas City Chiefs beat out Washington tight end Jordan Reed in the 2016 "Madden Bowl."

NFL Blitz

Unlike Madden's emphasis on replicating a realistic NFL experience, NFL Blitz is designed as a fast-paced, arcade-style video game alternative. Featuring two-minute quarters, no penalties, and seven-on-seven teams, NFL Blitz places importance on long pass plays, high scoring, and the ability to literally "catch on fire" when a player is having an excellent game. Players are exaggerated, larger-than-life characters with bulging muscles that more closely resemble superheroes than their real-life counterparts. In addition to playing as players from your favorite NFL team, you can also play as special characters like zombies, lions, and Bigfoot.

The Pro Football Hall of Fame

If you're a fan of the NFL, you will love a trip to the Hall of Fame in Canton, Ohio. Even though the players and teams that you'll see there probably played before you started following football, you'll still enjoy learning some of the football history you've heard about.

What's in There?

When you enter the building, you'll see an enormous room with a domed roof. In the middle is a life-sized statue of Jim Thorpe. In the galleries around the statue are some of the hall's most historically interesting displays, including:

- The shoe used to kick the longest field goal ever
- Jim Brown's helmet
- Walter Payton's game uniform from when he broke the all-time rushing record
- Y.A. Tittle's old-style helmet that was cracked in half during a game
- An enormous knee brace worn by Joe Namath

The other members of the Hall of Fame don't get full life-sized statues, but they do all get bronze busts of their heads. One large room contains all of these busts. The hall contains displays celebrating great players of the past and present. These displays may show a game uniform, a photo of a player in action, or a plaque summarizing his accomplishments. Many of the player displays are grouped by team.

The hall has a display of equipment worn by pro football players throughout history. You'll be amazed at the leather helmets without facemasks, the old-style shoulder

pads, and the strange-looking balls that were used in the 1920s. There are the actual jerseys worn by players when important events happened. For example, you can see the uniform LaDainian Tomlinson wore when he set the NFL's season touchdown record in 2006. The hall collects the footballs used in historic games and stores them in a huge room in shoeboxes on shelves.

How Are the Hall of Fame Players Chosen?

Hall of Fame players are chosen by a selection committee. Each team sends one representative to this committee. Usually this is the reporter from the local newspaper who follows the team. Throughout the year, the selectors talk by e-mail and vote to create a ballot of seventeen candidates for the year.

On the day before the Super Bowl, the whole committee meets to talk about that year's candidates. One person presents an argument for each. Once the discussion is over, the selectors vote. The players with the most support become members of the Hall of Fame. Each year, the selectors are required to choose at least three new Hall of Famers, but they can't choose more than six.

The ceremony that makes someone a member happens in July in Canton. The player is shown his bust, he's given a gold jacket, and he gets to make a speech. Lots of fans attend these ceremonies, but it's televised if you can't go.

Chapter 9
BEHIND THE SCENES

The Bosses on the Practice Field: The Coaching Staff

The head coach, especially the head coach of a major college or NFL team, is hardly behind the scenes. In fact, many bigtime head coaches host a weekly television show! Even high school head coaches are well-known near-celebrities in their communities. The assistant coaches and the coaches of the lower-level high school teams, though, are not household names. These folks work hard, too, but not many people (aside from the players and school community) are likely to know who they are or what they do.

College and Professional Assistant Coaches

Assistant coaches at the college and NFL level are career coaches, for the most part. They have decided that they want to learn how to be a bigtime coach, often (but not always) with the goal of becoming a head coach somewhere. Coaching is these folks' full-time job. Most assistants are position coaches, with one person in charge of linebackers, another for defensive backs, and so on. An assistant's role is to relate personally to each player he is in charge of and to help those players develop their skills. In season, assistant coaches must understand each game plan, then figure out how to teach their players to execute that plan. If an effective football team consists of lots of different units working together, then the assistant coaches are the ones who train each individual unit.

High School Assistant Coaches

At the high school level, most assistants are teachers at the school. At first, you may think it a bit strange to have teachers as football coaches, especially if they teach something like physics or art. It's not these teachers' academic knowledge that is useful on the football field as much as their teaching ability. Coaching, after all, is teaching: explaining techniques, motivating, helping players learn new and sometimes difficult approaches. Coaching is not a high school assistant's full-time job. But then football is not a high school player's full-time job, either. The players often develop an improved appreciation for their coaches' classes. They may not have enjoyed chemistry class before, but if the offensive line coach is also the chemistry teacher, they might find the subject more manageable.

Who Makes You Look Good: The Equipment Manager

The equipment manager is one of the most important of the support staff during the game. If someone's helmet breaks, he simply can't play unless someone, usually the equipment manager, fixes it. The equipment manager is also in charge of making sure every player's uniform is ready to go on game day.

Uniforms

Football is an all-weather outdoor sport. After a game, those great-looking uniforms become covered with grass stains, mud, and sweat. The equipment manager's main job is to get the uniforms clean for the next game. That's no mean task considering the average team has seventy to 100 sets of jerseys, pants, socks, and so on. Holes in jerseys have to be sewn back together. The uniforms go through the wash seven or eight times and are treated in between to help remove stains. When they're finally done, each complete uniform is assembled and hung in the correct player's locker. And there's more . . . much, much more. So much more, in fact, that a major college or NFL program has as many as ten to twenty people working under the supervision of the head equipment manager.

Equipment Staff Rituals

At Penn State University, the head equipment manager and staff spend every Thursday night before a game repairing and painting the players' black shoes. Then they clean and repair the players' white helmets. At Notre Dame, before each game the helmets receive a fresh coat of gold paint. Most every equipment staff has some kind of special pregame custom. Do you know the staff ritual of your favorite team?

While the laundry from last week's game is in the machines, the equipment managers get ready for the week's practices. Each team's specific routine is different, but the main idea is the same for all: get each player the correct practice jersey. This is more complicated than you might think. The team can't all look the same for practice because they have to have different-colored jerseys for offense and defense. Some teams have even more different outfits. Perhaps the starters and reserves wear different colors, too. The coaches might also have special requests. For example, if the next opponent wears green and has a really good linebacker who wears the number 50, the coaches might ask for one of their own scout team linebackers to wear a green number-50 jersey in practice. The equipment managers have to sort out the practice jerseys, giving the correct one to each player; then they have to have all the rest of the players' equipment ready, including helmets, pads, and shoes.

Heavy Lifting

While laundry and practice preparation are going on, the staff is still unpacking stuff from the previous week's game, cleaning, organizing, and repacking for the next week's game. During a game, things get damaged, broken, and lost. The equipment manager must be able to replace any piece of equipment instantly. That takes organization and planning. The team brings extra shoes, cleats, pants, mouthpieces, pads, and pretty much anything needed to keep every player available for the whole game. It takes a good part of a week's work to get all of this spare stuff in the right place, ready for travel to the game site.

Two or three days before an away game, the entire staff loads everything onto a huge truck. This truck drives to the game, arriving well before the team. The equipment managers themselves fly with the team, but they don't get to go right to the team hotel. They have to

Fancy Footwork

Break the letter and number equations to find the silly answer to the riddle.

Why did the official kick Cinderella out of the game?

FWEEP

A+4
I-1
P+3
X+1   G-2
I-4   B-1   F+2
R+1   T+3   V-2
V-1   D-3
D-3   J+3   J+2
A+2   M+1   L+3   N-2
G-2   E-4   S-1   D-3
G-5   P+2   D+2   A+1

Respecting the Student Managers

Unfortunately, sometimes there are players who don't understand how important and hard working the managers are. A good coach will not allow this behavior. Most coaches lecture the team at the beginning of the season about how to treat the managers respectfully. At the end of the year, the coaches make sure that the managers get the same kind of honors as the players do.

meet the truck and unload all of the equipment onto the sideline before they can rest.

The head equipment manager can work eighty-hour weeks during the season. That's crazy—forty hours per week is the standard for most workers! Taking care of a team's stuff is long, hard work, but it all pays off on game day.

Team Managers

Think about all the small jobs that need to be done to help out a football team. There are a lot of these. Someone needs to fill up water bottles before practice and during practice, then the water bottles need to be cleaned up and put away. What about the footballs themselves? Someone has to take charge of giving out balls to various coaches and players who need them for practice, then collecting them after practice, finding any that got thrown into the bushes, and putting them away where they belong.

Managers are critical to the team's success, so a good coaching staff will bend over backward to let them know their importance. Managers pack up for away games with the rest of the equipment staff. They prowl the sideline on game day, filling whatever role is needed. Some will fetch and (on bad-weather days) clean the game balls.

So You Want to Be a Manager?

Perhaps the best way for a young person to get involved with a football team is as a manager. High school teams have occasionally used managers as young as nine or ten. Even if you don't know anyone on the team, show up to practice a few times just to watch. Look carefully at what goes on and figure out something you could do to make practice go smoother for everyone. For example, maybe one of the coaches is having trouble carrying around his clipboard and running a drill at the same time. Before practice one day, go up to the coach and ask him if you could carry the clipboard for him. Start small, asking to do one or two specific things. During practice, try to be as quiet and useful as you can. If you're a hard worker who learns how the team operates, you'll be surprised how quickly you will be asked to take on more jobs. The coaches will come to rely on you to take care of things, so you'll be asked to come to the games to work. Ta-da—you're a student manager!

OW! The Athletic Trainer

Football is a hard-hitting game. After a game or a hard practice, every player, even the best-conditioned athlete, feels sore. Isn't it great that the athletic trainer is there, waiting to help you feel better?

The Athletic Trainer's Job

Most high school athletic programs have an athletic trainer who works with athletes in all their sports. Colleges and NFL football teams employ four or five trainers for their roster of sixty to ninety players. These trainers are all an integral part of the team. During the seven months of the season, these dedicated folks work seven days a week. They tape ankles and otherwise prepare every player for every practice. They help supervise rehabilitation. After practice, trainers help players ice, stretch, and otherwise assist their bodies start the recovery process so they'll be ready for the next practice.

Major injuries in football are, in fact, reasonably rare. Studies show that soccer players are considerably more likely to suffer serious injuries than football

players. Why? One of many reasons for the low injury rate is that football teams actively work to prevent injury. The athletic trainers supervise the stretching and taping that is an important part of injury prevention. Trainers also attend daily to all the nagging, minor soreness and strains that could become major injuries without treatment. And, of course, state-of-the-art protective equipment absorbs most of the hard hits.

NFL trainers travel with the team the day before a game. At the team hotel, the training staff takes over a big conference room to use as a training room. On game day, the trainers work nonstop. They open up their hotel training room as early as they wake up. Then they move all of their equipment to the game site. Several hours before the game, players begin to show up for pregame preparation. The trainers will spend at least five minutes per player taping ankles, stretching out tight muscles, covering protective casts, and making sure that every player's body is ready by game time.

During the game, the trainers spread out on the sideline with the team. They are instantly ready to deal with injuries, both major and minor. They (along with the team doctor) tell the coach which injured players can get back in the game and who needs to sit out. Game time is what the trainers live for. Even though they're not playing, they get the same rush of excitement as the players do because 70,000 fans are screaming for the team to win, and the trainers are part of that team.

The trainer's job never ends. Even on the plane ride home, trainers are giving out ice packs and making sure injured players are positioned correctly. Then, after everyone else has gone home, the trainers stick around for an extra hour or so with injured players to get treatment started right away.

Loads of Laundry

There are 48 jerseys to wash and repair before the next game. Figure out how many jerseys each of the five equipment managers is responsible for.

Jonas gets 13 jerseys.

Tom gets twice as many jerseys as Jean.

Jean gets as many jerseys as Lonny.

Lida gets 10 fewer jerseys than Jonas.

Jean gets 5 jerseys more than Lida.

Jonas
Tom
Jean
Lonny
Lida

So You Want to Be an Athletic Trainer?

First, you have to get a college degree. Ideally, you'd major in the physical or biological sciences, but there are also programs specifically in health, fitness, and exercise science. You can earn a master's or professional degree in athletic training and take some tests to become an officially certified trainer. Then you're ready to apply for a job. It's an intense job, but it's an awesome one, too.

Keeping a Clean Game: The Officials

There is a job you can do every weekend. You'll have to spend hours ahead of time getting ready: going to meetings, studying, and traveling. You have to pass a test to be allowed to do the job. When it's time to start, you'll be expected to sprint a total of several miles to keep up

Women Can Be Officials, Too

There is no rule anywhere that girls can't play football, but it's very rare to see a female player, usually because boys simply grow bigger and stronger. That said, there's absolutely no reason that a girl couldn't become an official. There are a fair number of female officials throughout the country. In 2015, after a long and successful NCAA career, Sarah Thomas joined Pete Morelli's crew as a line judge.

White Hat

Officials other than the referee wear black hats with teeny white stripes. The referee, though, wears a pure white hat. Among officials, the term "white hat" refers to the referee.

with people who are faster than you. You can expect to get knocked down occasionally by giants wearing armor. Everyone—maybe thousands of people—will complain about everything you do. They'll scream at you and call you names, even if you do a good job. When it's all over, you'll get paid. Woo-hoo! Go to the bookstore to spend your paycheck, and you'll be able to buy maybe two books. Such is the life of a football official.

Though they do hard work, football officials truly love what they are doing. For one thing, they know how critical they are to the game. Can you imagine a game without officials? That wouldn't work. Though fans and coaches will yell at them, most of them respect the tremendous effort that officials put into calling every game.

The people who officiate do so for many reasons. Many are former athletes who are too old to play anymore but who still love football and want to stay involved. Some might not have been good enough to play football but are extremely good at calling the game. Officials must be just as focused in their minds and their bodies as the players are during a game.

Most importantly, despite the craziness, officiating football can be fun. How many times have you watched a game on TV and wished you could be part of the action?

How to Become an Official

Start by finding a local officiating association. Find one on the Internet or talk to the referee before a game at a nearby high school. In most areas, officials join an association and then the association assigns them to local games. The higher-level games, and especially the playoff games, go to the best and most experienced people.

Talk to the person in charge. Depending on the sport and the locality, there are different requirements to meet before you're allowed to work games. You're almost definitely too young to work a game right now. But you're not too young to learn the rules and what are called the mechanics—where to go on the field, what to look for, and how to make a call. Let the people in the association give you advice on where to start.

Officiating Positions

Football officials work in teams. A junior varsity game might have four officials. The NFL and most college conferences use seven officials on a team. Every member of the team has a different job to do.

- The **referee** is the crew chief, supervising all the officials on the team. During the game, the referee stands behind the offense and is primarily responsible for watching the quarterback. He announces penalties to the coaches and the spectators.
- The **umpire** stands directly behind the defensive line. His job is to watch the blockers to make sure no one is holding. He also gets the ball ready for the next play.
- The **head linesman** and the **line judge** stand on the sideline, right on the line of scrimmage. They look to see that the play starts correctly, then they are responsible for any action near the sideline. The head linesman runs the chain crew, making sure they can measure for a first down if necessary.
- The **field judge**, **side judge**, and **back judge** start each play way behind the defense. They watch out for pass interference. They take over watching the action when a play goes for long yardage. Some leagues, especially in high school, only use a field judge, not a side or back judge.

STATS, LLC

STATS is a company that hires reporters to watch every college and NFL game to keep statistics. On game day, STATS provides live score updates to websites and television stations. Even video game programmers use the information collected by STATS to help make their games realistic.

Pro Football Reference

Perhaps the most comprehensive site for NFL statistics is *www.pro-football-reference.com*. Click on a game from this season, or any season since 1920(!). You'll get a box score, starters, complete play-by-play of the game, and even a chart estimating the chances of each team winning after each play. You can find single-season and all-time records in any category you might imagine. This is *the* site for a football stats enthusiast to get lost in.

The Statisticians Know More Than Just the Score

Have you ever heard a television broadcaster say something like, "That 8-yard run gives Frank Gore 286 yards on the day, third best ever behind Adrian Peterson and Jamal Lewis"? Well, it's not like the announcer added up Gore's yards in his head. At every football game, from the high school level to the NFL, one or more statisticians are keeping track of what happens on every play. These folks are the ones who know all the important numbers behind the game.

Statisticians at High School Games

A high school team usually asks a student, or perhaps a parent, to volunteer to keep statistics during its games. This person works either on the sideline or in the press box, writing down who carried or passed the ball and how many yards he gained on each play. He also writes down how each team scored touchdowns or field goals. At the end of the game, the statistician writes a box score; usually, this box score is then sent to a local newspaper to be published the next day.

After each game, the statistician also puts together the team's overall season stats. These are used at the end of the season to help decide who gets team or all-state awards.

Statisticians at College and NFL Games

There are so many football statistics that people like to know about. It's not hard for one volunteer to collect rushing and passing yardage. But other stuff is harder to keep track of. How many times did the team make it on third down? How many tackles did each defender make? How many penalties did the team commit, and how many yards did they cost? Some of these things can be figured out by scouts, by watching video of the game. But at the college and NFL level, fans want to know these things immediately as they watch on television. So, a lot of people work together to put together all of the stats.

Several people might be assigned to look at different parts of each play—one person for offense, one for defense, for example. Computers store the data, and do all the math so that people can see results right away. In the press box, screens are updated after each play with information from the statisticians. A television announcer can just look at this screen to see live stats.

The Scouts

Teams need to know about the team they're playing next. What kind of offense and defense do they run? Who are their best players? The strategies a team uses will depend on what they think the other team will do. Figuring out what the other team can do is called scouting.

In high school, scouting is usually done by just a few coaches watching video. College and NFL coaches also watch video of their opponents . . . but the higher the level of football, the more intense the scouting that goes on. Imagine that the NFL team that you coach is playing the Patriots next week. How do you get your game plan ready?

You'll use a whole lot of people to figure out how the Patriots play. First of all, you'll send people to this week's Patriots game. These folks will sit in the press box or the stands, making notes on what they see. How many seconds does it take for the punter to kick the ball? How far away does the field goal kicker make his warm-up kicks? How is Tom Brady talking to his receivers on the sideline? Which coach seems to be sending in the defensive plays? Any of these things might give you an idea to help you win next week.

Next, you'll look at what the statisticians say about the Patriots. These statisticians will record all kinds of

PLAY ACTION: A fake handoff to a running back before a quarterback tries to throw a pass is called "play action."

Watching "Film"?

Way back before your parents were born, the only way to see a recording of another team's game was to watch film projected like in a movie theater. Nowadays, coaches watch video on a computer or DVD player. So, why do they still usually call this "watching film"?

details about every Patriots play in every game, this year and in years past. How many defensive players lined up on the line of scrimmage? Which cornerback covered the strongest receiver? How often did they run play action? Maybe you can figure out a tip that might help you know whether a play is a running or a passing play, or what route a receiver will run.

And finally, you'll watch video, just like a high school coach. In the NFL, though, a staff of video coordinators will have used computer editing equipment to make video watching easier. Do you want to see all of the Patriots running plays to the right side on third down? Click a button. Would you rather see every play when Tom Brady threw a long pass? Just click. You can quickly see whatever kind of play you want.

So you see, while a game is played by only twenty-two players at a time, and for three or so hours once a week, lots and lots of people are working all week to make sure the game goes well. And each week, thousands of games are played, in high school, college, and the NFL. Is it any wonder that football is the most loved sport in America?

Appendix A

FOOTBALL FACTS AND RECORDS

The records football players hold help fans understand just how good they were.
Here are some of the important NFL individual career records:

Most NFL Rushing Yards

Emmitt Smith	Cowboys, Cardinals	18,355
Walter Payton	Bears	16,726
Barry Sanders	Lions	15,269
Frank Gore	Best Active Player as of 2016	12,040

Most Passing Yards

Peyton Manning	Colts, Broncos	71,940
Brett Favre	Packers, Falcons, Vikings, and others	71,838
Dan Marino	Dolphins	61,361

Most Receiving Yards

Jerry Rice	49ers, Raiders, Seahawks	22,895
Terrell Owens	49ers, Eagles, Cowboys, and others	15,934
Andre Johnson	Best Active Player as of 2016	14,100

Most Touchdowns Scored

Jerry Rice	49ers, Raiders, Seahawks	208
Emmitt Smith	Cowboys, Cardinals	175
LaDainian Tomlinson	Chargers, Jets	162
Antonio Gates	Best Active Player as of 2016	104

Most Points Scored

Morten Andersen	Saints, Falcons, and others	2,544
Gary Anderson	Steelers, Vikings, and others	2,434
Adam Vinatieri	Patriots, Colts	2,253
Jason Hanson	Lions	2,150

NFL Team Records

While individuals are important, football is a team game. Here are some NFL team records:

Most Super Bowl Victories

Steelers	6
Cowboys, 49ers	5

Most Super Bowls Played

Cowboys, Steelers, Patriots, Broncos	8
49ers	6

Most NFL Championships

Packers	12
Bears	9
Giants	7

College Team Records

It's tough to find meaningful college football records. Since there wasn't a multiteam playoff until 2014, each year might have several national champions. Individual statistics don't mean a lot either, since some teams schedule easy games to get players more yards gained. But here are some notable records:

Most National Championships since 1900

Alabama	15
Notre Dame	13
Michigan	11

Most Big Ten Championships

Michigan	42
Ohio State	35
Minnesota	18

Most Pac-12 Championships

Southern California	36
UCLA	17
Washington, Stanford	15

Most SEC Championships

Alabama	24
Tennessee	13
Georgia	12

Most Rose Bowl Victories

Southern California	24
Michigan	8
Washington, Ohio State	7

Most Orange Bowl Victories

Oklahoma	12
Nebraska	8
Miami	6

The Heisman Trophy

The Heisman is awarded each year to an outstanding college football player. Football writers and broadcasters vote for the winner. In recent years, winners have included Auburn's Cam Newton, Baylor's Robert Griffin III, Texas A&M's Johnny Manziel, and Florida State's Jameis Winston.

Most Heisman Trophies

Archie Griffin	Ohio State	2

Heisman Trophy winners who also made the Pro Football Hall of Fame include:

- Doak Walker, Southern Methodist
- Paul Hornung, Notre Dame
- Roger Staubach, Navy
- O.J. Simpson, Southern California
- Tony Dorsett, Pittsburgh
- Earl Campbell, Texas
- Marcus Allen, Southern California
- Barry Sanders, Oklahoma State

Heisman Trophy winners who are playing in the NFL as of the 2016 season include:

- Cam Newton, Auburn—quarterback for the Panthers
- Mark Ingram, Alabama—running back for the Saints
- Sam Bradford, Oklahoma—quarterback for the Rams and Eagles
- Reggie Bush, Southern California—running back for the Saints, Dolphins, and Lions
- Carson Palmer, Southern California—quarterback for the Bengals, Raiders, and Cardinals
- Jameis Winston, Florida State—quarterback for the Buccaneers
- Marcus Mariota, Oregon—quarterback for the Titans

Appendix B

GLOSSARY

Athletic scholarship:
Money given to a college athlete to pay for tuition and living expenses.

Ball security:
Holding on to the ball correctly so as not to fumble.

Blackout:
If an NFL game is not sold out three days ahead of time, the game cannot be shown on TV in the home team's city.

Blitz:
When more than four defensive players rush the quarterback.

Bye:
A week when a team doesn't play a game. NFL teams get one bye each season.

Chain gang:
The people who carry a chain to indicate the line for the next first down.

Coffin corner:
A punt that goes out of bounds near (but not in) the end zone.

Commissioner:
The person in charge of a league. The commissioner of the NFL is Roger Goodell. A fantasy league also appoints a commissioner.

Contain:
The defensive line tries to keep, or contain, the quarterback in the pocket.

Crossing routes:
When receivers run routes with crossing paths, designed to confuse a zone defense.

Defense:
The part of a football team that tries to stop the offense from scoring.

Draw play:
A running play that starts after the defense thinks it's a passing play.

Eligible receiver:
Anyone who is allowed to catch a pass. This usually includes everyone except the five offensive linemen.

Flea flicker:
A trick play. The running back is handed the ball and starts to run but throws the ball back to the quarterback who throws a long pass to a receiver.

Holding:
Unless he's trying to tackle the ballcarrier, no one is allowed to grab, hug, or tackle. Holding results in a 10-yard penalty.

Homecoming:
The game when the school's graduates come back to watch and celebrate.

Home-field advantage:
For a lot of reasons, the home team wins about 60 percent of all NFL games.

Hot route:
A route run by a receiver for when the defense blitzes.

Independents:
College football teams that do not belong to a conference.

Lateral:
A backward pass. Any player can throw a lateral at any time.

Luxury box:
A fancy room in a football stadium with food, drinks, and nice furniture.

Merger, The:
In 1970, the American Football League and the National Football League came together to form a single NFL.

NFL:
These initials stand for National Football League. This is the most successful professional sports league in the world.

Offense:
The part of a football team that controls the ball and tries to score.

On an island:
When a cornerback has to cover a receiver man-to-man without help.

Pass interference:
A penalty called when the defensive player hits a receiver while a pass is in the air.

Play:
A play starts when the center snaps the ball; a play ends when the ballcarrier is tackled or goes out of bounds.

Pocket:
The area where the quarterback stands to throw a pass.

Redshirt:
Sitting out for a year to gain an extra year of eligibility for a college football player.

Sack:
When the quarterback wants to pass but is tackled behind the line of scrimmage.

Screen pass:
A short pass designed to fool the defense.

Single wing:
A formation, rarely used today, with lots of tight linemen to help run the football.

Snap count:
The number of "Hut!"s that the quarterback says before the snap.

T formation:
An offensive formation that puts the quarterback under center with three running backs behind the quarterback.

Tackle:
Making the ballcarrier fall to the ground. The offensive linemen who line up outside the guards. The defensive linemen who line up closest to the ball.

Tailgating:
Having a cookout or a party in the parking lot before a football game.

Touchback:
A kick or a punt that enters the end zone, allowing the offense to take possession on the 20-yard line.

Two-a-days:
Preseason practices that happen twice a day.

West Coast offense:
A passing offense that features short passing routes.

Wild card:
A team that makes the playoffs but didn't win its division.

YAC:
Stands for yards after catch, the yardage that a receiver gains after he catches the ball.

Appendix C
PUZZLE ANSWERS

FIND THE FLAG • page 9

WAY TO PLAY • page 19

I | PLAY | TWO
POSITIONS-
FIRST | I'M
CROUCHED
DOWN, | THEN
I'M | UP | AND
RUNNING !

WOOFBALL • page 15

A GOLDEN RECEIVER!

LOST PLAYER • page 25

Why did the football coach shake the vending machine?

H E | W A N T E D | H I S
Q U A R T E R | B A C K !

Where you wear a glove
H A N D
9 20 5 8

Opposite of loud
Q U I E T
12 13 10 2 6

Opposite of dry
W E T
3 7 16

Piece of equipment
that stops a car
B R A K E
19 15 14 22 17

What happens when
a car doesn't stop
C R A S H
21 18 4 11 1

FIND THE FOOTBALL • page 28

```
T A B O O L O F
F O O T T O B A O L O O
B F O O F O F O O T T B A L L
T A O L F L O O F O O B L A L F
F O O T B F O O O T B A L A L O O F
F O O T O L T A O B B O L F L F L O A B
F O O B T L L A B T O O F B O F T O
B A A O F O O T T O F B A L F O
F L O T B A F O L O F O T O
L F O O T A O A O L L O
T O O L B A T O
```

FRACTURED FOOTBALL • page 40

BRUSH UP • page 30

```
Y O U   A R E   S U C H   A
G O O D   P L A Y E R   T H A T
E V E N   Y O U R   B R E A T H
    I S   O F F E N S I V E !
```

FOOTBALL FILL IN • pages 44–45

PERFECT PLAY • page 33

SUPER SIZED • page 50

The one with the biggest head!

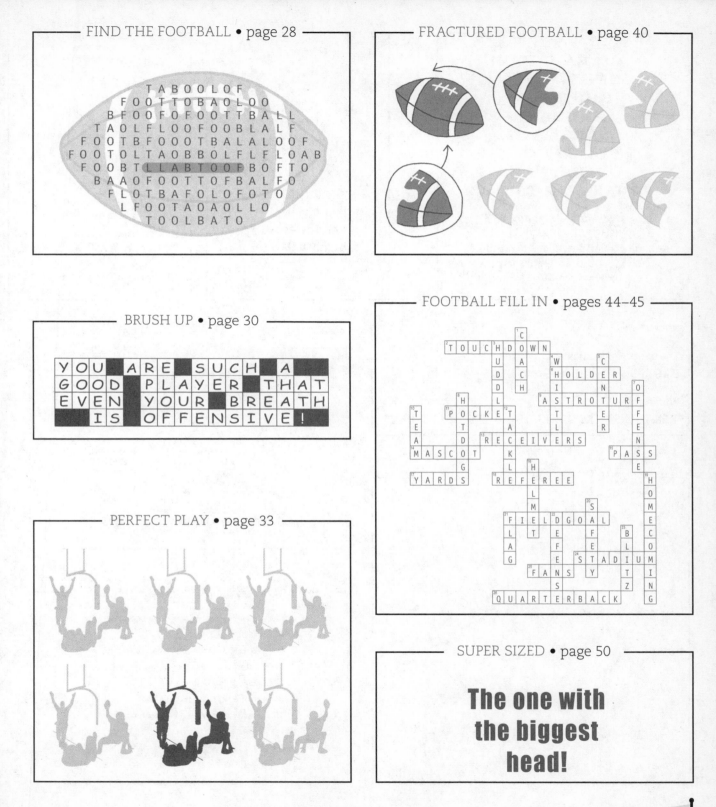

141

RAH, RAH, RAH!
SKI-U-MAH,
HOO-RAH!
HOO-RAH!
VARSITY!
VARSITY!
VARSITY,
MINN-E-SO-TAH!

"Ski-U-Mah" is pronounced SKY-YOU-MAH. "Ski" is a Native American battle cry meaning "victory." "U-Mah" represents the <u>U</u>niversity of <u>M</u>innesota.

What is the difference between a football player and a duck?

· · · · · · · · · · · · ·

You'll find one in a huddle, and the other in a puddle!

lunch wrappers and empty lunch bag
T R A <u>S</u> H

mistake in Drivers' Ed.
C R A <u>S</u> H

important to have in chorus
B R E <u>A</u> <u>T</u> H

art project with dried flowers
<u>W</u> R E <u>A</u> T H

what boring teachers do
P R E <u>A</u> C H

activity in math class
G R A <u>P</u> H

after-school fundraiser
C A <u>R</u> <u>W</u> A <u>S</u> H

The most popular mascots are:
EAGLES BULLDOGS TIGERS LIONS

Some more unusual mascots are:
PENGUINS KANGAROOS OWLS BLUE HENS

IF	~~TENNIS~~	TWO	~~DISC~~
~~GOLF~~	FLIES	ARE	~~BASKETBALL~~
~~DISHES~~	~~CLOSET~~	~~JOG~~	~~SKI~~
IN	~~VOLLEYBALL~~	THE	~~HAMPER~~
~~SPIKES~~	KITCHEN	~~HAMPER~~	WHICH
~~SOCCER~~	ONE	~~BUDDIES~~	~~UP~~
IS	~~OAR~~	THE	~~PING-PONG~~
~~BADMINTON~~	FOOTBALL	~~NET~~	PLAYER

1. Is the game on one di**sc or el**even cassettes?
2. We won! Hear us "Hoo**ray!**"
3. The cham**p lay** winded in the end zone.
4. The quarterback **spun,** then threw the ball.
5. Tired player**s nap** before a big game.
6. Don't panic! **Lock** the stadium door!
7. All I need is to move the ball four more yards!
8. Losing teams **weep** in private.
9. All of Ray **Spigs' kin** came to watch him play!
10. Drinking iced **tea** makes players less thirsty.

RUN LIKE CRAZY • page 84

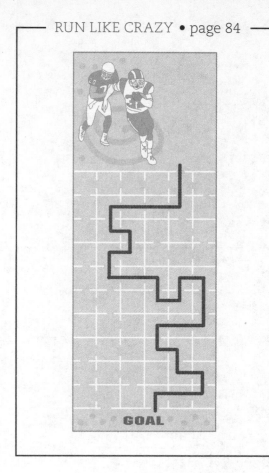

GOAL

WACKY WEATHER • page 113

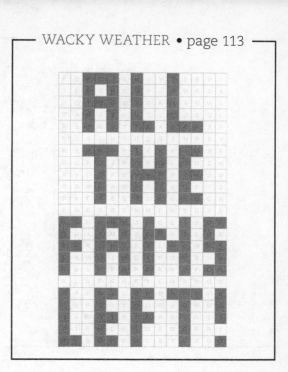

ALL THE FANS LEFT!

MOST VALUABLE PLAYER • page 95

"Hey, Coach! I want to play
<u>END</u>, <u>GUARD</u>, and <u>TACKLE</u>."

"OK — <u>SIT</u> at the <u>END</u> of the
<u>BENCH</u>, <u>GUARD</u> the <u>WATER</u>
<u>BUCKET</u>, and <u>TACKLE</u>
<u>ANYONE</u> who gets <u>NEAR</u> it!"

ALL MIXED UP • page 114

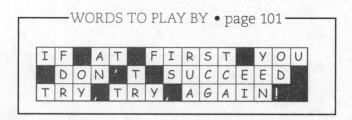

A H X W

Imagine that
a fantasy
owner has players
from two
different teams.
When both "real"
teams play each
other, the
fantasy owner
will hope that
both teams
score a lot!

WORDS TO PLAY BY • page 101

I	F		A	T		F	I	R	S	T		Y	O	U
D	O	N	'	T		S	U	C	C	E	E	D		
T	R	Y	,		T	R	Y	,		A	G	A	I	N	!

143

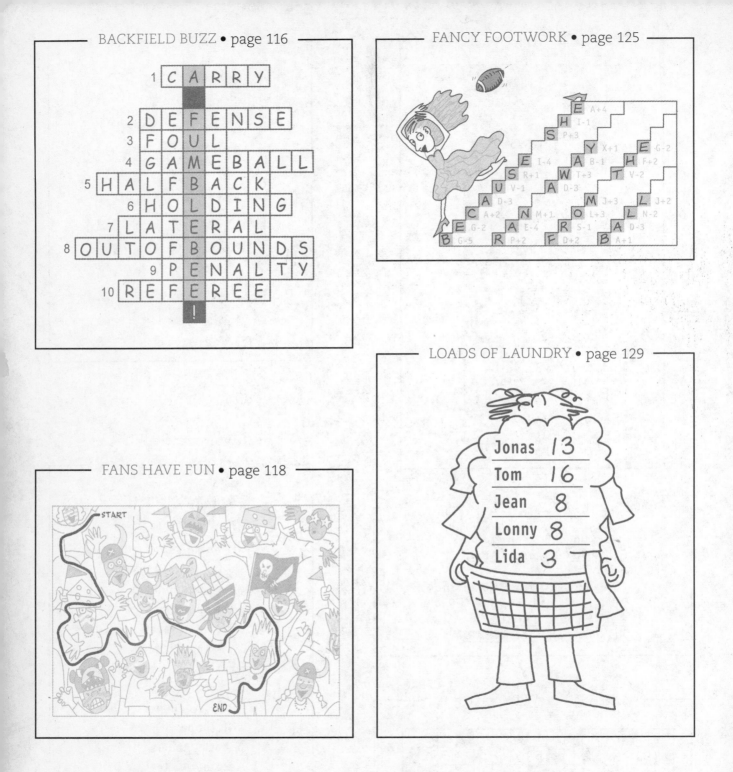

Jonas	13
Tom	16
Jean	8
Lonny	8
Lida	3